Jewish Magic and Kabbalah

A Guide to Ancient Hebrew Mysticism and Hermetic Qabalah

Free Bonus from Silvia Hill available for limited time

Hi Spirituality Lovers!

My name is Silvia Hill, and first off, I want to THANK YOU for reading my book.

Now you have a chance to join my exclusive spirituality email list so you can get the ebooks below for free as well as the potential to get more spirituality ebooks for free! Simply click the link below to join.

P.S. Remember that it's 100% free to join the list.

~~$27~~ FREE BONUSES

- 9 Types of Spirit Guides and How to Connect to Them

- How to Develop Your Intuition: 7 Secrets for Psychic Development and Tarot Reading

- Tarot Reading Secrets for Love, Career, and General Messages

Access your free bonuses here
https://livetolearn.lpages.co/jewish-magic-and-kabbalah-paperback/

Table of Contents

Part 1: Jewish Magic

Unlocking Everything You Need to Know about Jewish Spirituality, Mysticism, and Angels

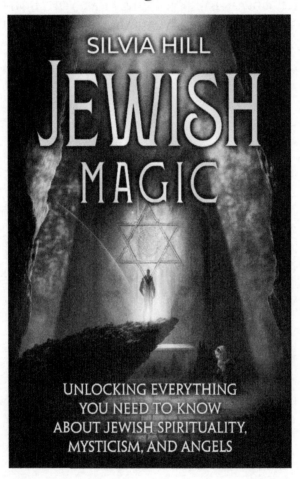

Introduction

This book is a comprehensive resource on Jewish spirituality, mysticism, and angels. If you've always wanted to learn about Jewish magic but needed to figure out where to begin, this is it. You might be interested in your Hebrew heritage, full of mystical magic. Or you may simply be interested in those aspects of occult knowledge rooted in Jewish spirituality or the Qabalah and want to learn as much as possible on the topic. It could be that you're just interested in starting your spiritual journey, and this is the path calling you the most. Whatever the case, you'll find the information you need on these pages.

Unlike other books on the market, this book is written clearly in plain English with no typos or grammatical errors, so there's no chance you'll misinterpret or misunderstand the message. You will not be left confused and scratching your head about what the concepts mean. By reading this book, you get the chance to look through expert eyes, get an accurate take on Jewish mysticism and spirituality, and dive into their rich history. You'll also be provided with daily routines and practices you can use to help you make the concepts very practical and real in your life. In addition, the writing is inclusive and respectful of cultural and ethnic backgrounds and gender.

This book is a beautiful resource because you'll get information far beyond what you'll find on the internet. It doesn't just dabble in the basics but dives deep into the treasures held in Jewish mysticism's depths. You'll appreciate the many fascinating things about Jewish magic as you read. It's not easy to find books written in English that cover the history of Hebrews and their practices, so you can consider this one a great find – an exceptional read compared to other books on the market!

There's much to explore in the world of Jewish magic and much that will change your life for the better in ways you couldn't possibly have anticipated. That's why your decision to choose this book, learn what it has to offer, and implement it in your life will serve you greatly. Many choose to flounder through life, never questioning it, never looking for meaning and purpose. You, dear reader, are clearly different. You recognize there's so much more to existence than meets the eye, and you've clearly taken the bold step to explore your spirituality.

Now, as you open this book to read, your path will open and light up for you to walk in it. If you're ready to connect to the power that lies in the secrets of Jewish mysticism, and you're ready to leave the person you are behind for a grander version of yourself, let's begin this journey with an introduction to Jewish mysticism and spirituality.

Chapter 1: Jewish Mysticism and Spirituality 101

Judaism is one of the oldest religions in the world, focusing on serving just one God. It begins as far back as 4,000 years, at least. Those who subscribe to this religion believe that God made himself known through the prophets of old. To understand Jewish mysticism, you must understand the history. There's much to cover regarding tradition, culture, and law.

Judaism is one of the oldest religions.

For the Jewish people, there's only one God, and God entered into a binding agreement with them, so they are God's chosen ones. God reaches out to those who believe in him through his prophets, rewarding those who do well and giving those who don't do well their due. Traditionally, being Jewish is passed down through the matriarchs of the family, which means if your mom is Jewish, so are you. If you're going to be a practicing Jew, you have to know about and study the *Tanakh,* which is the Hebrew Bible. This text is as sacred as the Quran to Muslims or the Bible to Christians. There are similarities between the Tanakh and the Christian Bible, specifically the Old Testament. Among the most important books of the Hebrew Bible are the collection known as the Torah, which is the first five books – or the *Pentateuch.* They are considered very important because they all have the important laws that one must follow if they are born or decide to be a Jew. What is one of the most important tenets of being a Jew? Judaism involves the belief that the Messiah will one day arrive to save his people. To serve God, you have to attend services at the synagogue, and the rabbi leads each service. Judaism is a way of life that is heavy with symbolism, and perhaps one of the most notable symbols is the six-pointed Star of David, which is universally recognized as Jewish. There's nearly nowhere you can't find Jews, as there are at least 14 million of them across all nations! Mostly, many of them are in their homeland, Israel. The only other place that is as populated by Jews as Israel is the United States of America.

Origins

Abraham was a Hebrew from the Old Testament times. However, he was no ordinary Hebrew; he was the one to whom God chose to reveal himself. Not only *that*, he was the one God made a remarkable promise: Abraham would be the father of all nations. That was a promise God made good on!

Abraham is the one who is, according to the Torah, who premiered the faith of Judaism. God entered into a contract or covenant with Abraham, promising that he and his offspring would become a powerful nation. Abraham had a son named Isaac and a grandson named Jacob. These three would go on to become very important personalities in Jewish history. Eventually, Jacob would take on a new name: Israel. The name Israel means "God contended," and he got that name after wrestling with an angel standing in for Yahweh. Obviously, wrestling with an angel was no mean feat, but somehow, Jacob could pull it off and survive. It's known that battling with God is a daily experience as you struggle with the process of asking questions and studying more, all to understand the great Ein Sof, and to find meaning in your life. Being a Jew doesn't mean you swallow everything you're taught hook, line, and sinker. You have to think about what you're being told of God for you to meet God within yourself. Just because you have questions about the things you learn about God doesn't make you a bad Jew. It took a thousand years after Abraham's time for the people of Israel to finally win their freedom from the tough enslavement of the Egyptians, and they couldn't have done this without God's help. He was able to rescue them through his holy servant, Moses. It was through Moses that the Oral Torah or Oral Law was made known to the Israelites, as God told Moses everything the people needed to know on Mount Sinai. The Jews have had some tough times all through history, with some events being so ugly that it was evident the faith and its details were in danger of being obliterated on account of systemic persecution. So a certain Rabbi known as Judah the Prince decided not to let that happen, and he wrote down everything of the Oral Torah in the Mishnah. The Mishnah is the first main collection of Jewish oral traditions that were penned down and the very first important work in rabbinic literature.

There are two very important figures in the history of Israel and Judaism: David and his son Solomon. David was the King of Israel at a certain point in time, and his son was the one who built the first Temple of Jerusalem, which was no mean feat. This meant that the Israelites finally had a formal place of worship where they could serve God. However, this Temple wasn't meant to last, as the kingdom of Israel would come to an end eventually. This meant that Israelites were now divided into two camps. In the North were Israelites, and in the South were the people of Judah. This split in the kingdom came around 931 BC, with the destruction of the first Temple happening in 587 BC. The Babylonians swooped in and destroyed everything the Israelites loved about their temple, and as if that weren't enough, they had to exile them as well. 71 years later, there would be a Second Temple, which only lasted a few centuries. Once more, the people were attacked, and their beloved place of worship was desecrated and destroyed, this time by the Romans. By 70 AD, the Second Temple was no more. This was a landmark event because it meant the Jews had nowhere to gather in worship, so they opted to continue their services in the local synagogues.

Historically, Jews have often been persecuted because of their beliefs. The following are some of the most terrible persecutions that they've had to endure:

- **The Granada Massacre of 1066:** The Granada Royal palace was situated in the Taifa of Granada. This was the place that a mob of Muslim faithfuls decided to break into. Joseph ha-Nagid was the Jewish vizier at the time, working with Berber taifa king Badis al-Muzaffar as, at the time, the Moors reigned over Al-Andalus, and the mob made sure to crucify him because he was the religious head of the Jews in the area. At the time, Spain was under the rulership of Muslims, specifically the Zirid dynasty. It is believed that Jews were in Granada ever since the First Temple was destroyed, and in fact, the place was once called Garnata-al-Yahud, which means Granada, the City of Jews. The Muslims were simply unhappy with the prosperity of the Jewish community at the time,

- **The First Crusade:** During this terrible event, crusaders made their way to Jerusalem, attacking the Jews they encountered as they went through Rhineland and the areas around Heidelberg. The crusaders made sure the Jews had only one of two options: Death or conversion. So many Jews were forced to end their lives with their own hands because they didn't want to betray God or their ways. This was just one in a series of anti-Semitic attacks that would build up to the Holocaust.

- **The Spanish Expulsion:** In 1492 royal edict issued by the Spaniard rulers said all Jews who wouldn't become Christians would be forced out of the country. They followed through on that threat, as about 200,000 Jews were expelled, and tens of thousands died trying to find somewhere safe to escape.

- **The Holocaust:** This is one of the most disastrous of events, as 6 million Jews were murdered in cold blood by the Nazis.

The Different Movements in Judaism

There are variations in the practice of Judaism, most of which are originally from Rabbinic Judaism. Here are the important movements to note.

Pharisaic Judaism is practiced by Pharisees, who had a movement in the Levant during the epoch of Second Temple Judaism. When the Second Temple was destroyed, the beliefs of the Pharisees made up the basis for Rabbinic Judaism.

Rabbinic Judaism is also known as Rabbinicism or Rabbinism. It's been the main form of Judaism since the 6th century CE, once the Babylonian Talmud. These Jews believe that Moses received God's Oral Torah and Written Torah. This form of Judaism holds the Oral Torah in high esteem, unlike the Sadducees, Samaritans, and Karaite Jews.

The Sadducees do not accept the Oral Torah but the Written Torah only. They believe there's no fate and God is incapable of committing evil. They also believe that man has free will, immortality doesn't exist, and there's no afterlife. They also don't believe in being rewarded or punished after death, nor in the resurrection of the dead.

Hellenistic Judaism is a combination of Greek culture and Jewish religious tradition. This was popular in Antioch, Syria, and Alexandria, Egypt, before the Muslim conquests happened.

Karaism or Karaite Judaism recognizes only the written Torah, and they have the Sevel Ha Yerushah, which is "the Yoke of Inheritance," which they have always passed down from the time of their ancestors till now.

Orthodox Judaism teaches that the rabbinical interpretations of the Torah are to be followed to the letter. There are over 600 rules meant to show Orthodox Jews how to comport themselves daily.

Conservative Judaism holds that the Jewish law and tradition have authority thanks to the people and the community, stemming from generations of accepted practices and not rooted in the divine revelation of the Torah.

Hasidic Judaism has followers known as the Hasidim, which means "the pious ones." It took over Eastern Europe to the point that at least half of the Jews in the region were Hasidic. This movement was led by Yisroel ben Eliezer, or Ba'al Shem Tov. Unfortunately, many Hasidic Jews were massacred during the Holocaust. Hasidic Judaism is a form of Judaism that arose when the Jews were persecuted. At this time, the Jews of Europe turned toward studying the Talmud for themselves and felt like

Judaism was being viewed only mostly through academic lenses, taking away from the spiritual aspect of it that makes it a joy to practice. They would gather in small groups, and these meetings took place in a shtiebel – a house of prayer. Here, they could worship and celebrate and socialize with one another.

Reform Judaism is also called Liberal Judaism or Progressive Judaism. This form acknowledges that faith is ever-evolving, and it is more about the ethics of the religion than the ceremony. Those practicing this form of Judaism believe that divine truth is constantly revealed and involves human logic. In other words, it's not just about the theophany Moses experienced on Mount Sinai. It doesn't belabor rituals and considers the body of Jewish laws or halakha optional.

An Overview of Jewish Spirituality

Judaism is rooted in the belief that there is only one God and that God cares what we do as humans. Remember, Abraham had been promised that he'd be the father of all nations, and since this promise was made by God himself, there was no way it would be broken. Since the people that sprung from Abraham's lineage were a direct consequence of the promise, God only wanted one thing from them, and that was for them to worship him. For the Jew, worshipping God is about being a caretaker for all of life in the same way God is a caretaker for the world he created. God told them they had to love one another the same way he loves the world. These two commandments are the major ones God requires the Israelites to follow, but there are other commandments and laws that they have to abide by to keep up their end of the covenant that he had with their forefather, Abraham. This covenant is what acts as the root of Judaism. There is an esoteric aspect to Judaism that some regard as everyday mysticism, and it is known as Kabbalah. Kabbalah is about the way you personally relate with God working with natural Jewish methods by observing the halakha, which is Jewish law. It's also about observing the Birkat Ha-Mitzvot, so that the Jew can become so close to God as to become one with him. The halakha is meant to be a way to help Jews get closer to God and draw the world closer to his divine power.

The Torah

The Torah.

Torah means "Law," "Instruction," or "Teaching." The first five books of the Hebrew Bible are what make up the Torah. The books are:

- Genesis
- Exodus
- Leviticus
- Numbers
- Deuteronomy

Since there are five books in the Torah, it is also known as the Pentateuch. It's also called the Written Torah, in the form of a scroll when it's used liturgically (as the Sefer Torah). The Torah is also known as the Chumash when it's in the form of a bound book, and it will often come with perushim, which are commentaries from Rabis.

Sometimes, Torah can represent the entirety of the Tanakh or the Hebrew Bible. In this case, one refers not just to the Pentateuch but all 24 books. Torah can also sometimes represent everything about Jewish culture, teaching, and practice, including texts from the Bible and inserts from Rabbis, which make up the Oral Torah. It is hard to have an unequivocal definition of the Torah since there are infinite faces to it and myriad ways to interpret it.

Mitzvah

In Jewish tradition, bar and bat mitzvah rituals mark the coming of age. Boys have bar mitzvah, while girls have bat mitzvah. The plural form is known as b'nei mitzvah, and when the ceremony is meant for more than one gender, that's what it's called. If it's only girls involved, then the correct term is b'not mitzvah. What is the essence of this event? It marks the fact that the parents are no longer held accountable for their children's thoughts, words, and actions, since they are now old enough to make their own choices and deal with the outcomes. When Jewish kids are that age, they become a bat mitzvah or bar mitzvah and are therefore responsible for their actions. Usually, the father of a bat mitzvah or bar mitzvah is meant to thank God for no longer needing to take on the children's punishments for their misbehavior or sin.

Girls become bat mitzvah at 12, while boys become bar mitzvah at 13 in Orthodox communities. Regarding Conservative, Reconstructionist, and Reform Judaism, the children make that transition at age 13, regardless of gender. This age is when the children are expected to have an understanding of Jewish norms and ritual law, as well as ethics. They are also eligible to participate in any part of Jewish community life that they want to, the same way the grown-ups in the community do.

Teshuvah

Teshuvah means "Repentance" and is an important aspect of Judaism, for it is the atonement for sins one commits. It is known and accepted that no one is perfect and that every now and then, people will sin. However, Judaism holds that you can reduce how often you sin in the future or stop sinning altogether by repenting for the evil you've done in the past. So, the main gold of repentance in Judaism is to encourage the transformation of oneself through ethics. One who chooses to represent Judaism is a Baal teshuva, and this person is considered even more honorable than one who is righteous or has no sin.

The Talmud, a major text of Rabbinic Judaism and the foundation of halakha, states that God created repentance even before the world as we know it. It's believed that you should repent right away. There's a Talmudic parable that Rabbi Eliezer taught those who followed him: "Repent one day before your death." Clearly, being able to forecast one's death is impossible, so the followers naturally asked how they were supposed to know when they'd be passing on. In response, the Rabbi said, "All the more reason, therefore, to represent today, lest one die tomorrow." Jews believe in the Divine judgment of God and that God is always willing to accept those who repent, particularly from the start of Elul (a month) all the way to the High Holiday season (also known as the Days of Awe or the High Holy Days, also called the Yamim Noraim). These holidays include the Day of Judgment or Rosh HaShanah, the Ten Days of Repentance or Aseret Yimei Teshuva, and the Day of Atonement or Yom Kippur. The Kabbalah also includes one more holiday, known as the Hoshana Rabbah.

Repentance involves acknowledging you've sinned, choosing to forsake the path of sin, being concerned about the consequences of your sin, being humble, acting in ways opposite to the sin, confessing the sin and asking for atonement, making amends, self-restraint, and so on.

Brit

Brit is a ceremony for Jewish boys that takes place when they are eight days old. This ceremony is also known as brit shel Avraham Avinu, which means "the covenant of Abraham, our Father." It is named after Abraham, the first recipient of the circumcision mitzvah. Brit literally means "chain," "ring," or "circle," and these infer the idea of a binding covenant between God and his people. Brit is at the very center of Judaism.

The creator God entered into covenants with Abraham, Isaac, and Jacob, as well as the Israelites on Mount Sinai and the Moabite planes as they were preparing to enter Israel itself. The brit is fundamentally Jewish, and it came about when everyone was willing to let other people live their lives the way they thought fit. It developed during a time when people would negotiate existence, agreeing that not only would they be loyal to their fellow Jew, but they would also help one another. This mutual assistance ensures that everyone in the community achieves much more than they possibly could on their own. It's not something one practices only when they are in the mood, but it is a core part of being Jewish. An example of brit would be marriage, for instance. Another brit is the Brit Bein HaBetarim, also known as the Covenant of Parts. This is the covenant God made with Abraham's descendants about moving from being oppressed and enslaved strangers in a foreign land to being in their land, the Land of Canaan (Israel).

The Kabbalah and Halakhah

Halakhah comes from halakha, a root word meaning "to go." It represents the laws of Judaism, separate from the Haggadah, which is the nonlegal aspect of the religion. It's all about the relationships that you have on a personal, interpersonal, national, and international level. It's also about the different observances and practices followed by Jews. The Bible talks about what it means to live a good life, phrasing it this way: "and shalt show them the way wherein they are to go and the work that they must do." At first, the word Halakhah (plural halakhot) referred to specific laws that were given in specific situations, such as the law handed to Moses by God on Sinai (Halakhah le-Moshe mi-Sinai). This meaning still persists, but now, it does so along with the one encompassing the Jewish laws and practices.

During the rabbinic period, the study of the halakha became very important. Since it is such a difficult subject to get into and equally important for living your life as a practicing Jew, it is deemed very important to study this more than any other aspect of the Jewish religion. It is generally assumed that the halakha goes all the way back to the time of Moses, excluding the elaborations and innovations added later in line with the new situations of the newer times. The halakha is rooted in Oral Torah.

Kabbalah means "tradition," "correspondence," or "reception." It refers to a Jewish school of thought. Those who follow this school of thought are known as Mekubbal. The kabbalah's definition depends on the goals of those who follow its ways and their tradition. The Jewish Kabbalah shows followers how the eternal God who never changes is connected to the world that never stops changing, which all humans live and are a part of. It is the relationship between the Infinite — Ein Sof — and all else. If you want to understand what the Kabbalah is all about, then you have to dive deep into classical Judaism scriptures. These scriptures are rooted in a set of spiritual writings known collectively as the Zohar. Sometimes, Kabbalah is also interpreted as "occult knowledge" or "mysticism." It's about the part of Judaism that covers all things related to who God is. Kabbalists believe that God's ways are mysterious, but they also understand that one can obtain true knowledge and understanding of that which is shrouded in mystery. They believe that by obtaining this information, one can become intimate with God. Kabbalists see God and his creation as one and the same instead of considering them separate beings. They have a strong desire to connect with God.

According to the Kabbalah, a part of God is enshrined in each person's soul, waiting to come to light. Divinity is in all things that exist, and therefore there's nothing but divinity all around us. The sacred teachings of the Kabbalah are understood through investigation to discover hidden meanings, oral transmission from a master Kabbalist, or direct revelation. The latter involves spirit possession, angel visitations, and other supernatural occurrences. The Kabbalah calls on one and all to experience God in spirit and truth, not just to know about God. This task can be done through rituals meant to give followers power and through the use of this power to create changes in the physical world and the worlds beyond.

Can Anyone Follow Jewish Spirituality?

Yes, you can follow Jewish spirituality. Just because practitioners don't try to convert people, you'll find that Judaism is open to one and all today. Conversion makes you as much a Jew as those who were born to Jewish mothers. The Biblical Ruth isn't just King David's great-great-grandmother but was also a convert to Judaism. The thing about conversions is that they tend to be accepted based on the Jewish community in question. For the most part, Orthodox Jews are very strict about where and how conversions are carried out and hardly endorse liberal Jewish conversions. Orthodox Jews may not accept your conversion as valid if it's done by a non-Orthodox institution because, for the most part, they don't consider non-Orthodox rabbis as actual rabbis. However, this shouldn't stop you from wanting to convert to Judaism and doing so.

Chapter 2: Sacred Jewish Symbols

This chapter will teach you about the most important Jewish symbols, their meaning, and why they matter. These symbols have some history. Some of them are more for religious practice, while others are more spiritual and cultural in nature.

The Menorah

The menorah is the representation of universal enlightenment and Talmudic wisdom. This candelabra has seven lamps, representing all seven branches of human knowledge. Six lamps bend inwards and are guided by the middle lamp, representing God's light. The menorah also represents that creation took place in seven days, and the middle lamp represents the Sabbath, on which no work takes place, and no sin is committed.

The Menorah.

Edmund Gall, CC BY-SA 2.0 <https://creativecommons.org/licenses/by-sa/2.0>, via Wikimedia Commons https://commons.wikimedia.org/wiki/File:Model_of_the_Menorah_Temple_-next_to_the_Temple_Institute.jpg

While the previous menorah is known as the Talmudic menorah, the Hanukkah menorah has nine branches, not seven. A fascinating thing happened when the Jewish Temple was destroyed by the West Asian Seleucid Empire. You see, the lams in the Temple had to be lit by specially prepared olive oil that was consecrated for that purpose only. However, much of it was destroyed, leaving only enough for the eternal flame to burn for a day and no more. So there was simply no hope that the flame wouldn't die out. However, a miracle happened. Day after day, the flame continued to burn with the reserved oil, and it was only used up by the eighth day, at which time there was now fresh oil to keep the flame burning. According to the Talmud, the seven-flamed menorah must only be used within the Temple walls.

The Dreidel

The Dreidel.
Adiel lo, CC BY-SA 3.0 <https://creativecommons.org/licenses/by-sa/3.0>, via Wikimedia Commons https://commons.wikimedia.org/wiki/File:Colorful_dreidels.JPG

The dreidel is also known as the dreidl or dreidle. It's a spinning top with four sides, often played during Hanukkah. It's like the Jewish version of the European teetotum, a gambling toy. All four faces of the dreidel have a Hebrew letter on them. The letters are:

- Nun
- Gimel
- Hei
- Shin

Nun means "nothing," gimel means "whole," hei means "half," and shin means "put in." Etymologically speaking, these letters stand in for the phrase "nes gadol haya sham," or "a great miracle happened there." This is about the Miracle of Hanukkah, where the oil lasted longer than was expected. There's a different phrase that is used, which is "nes gadol haya po," (which has the same meaning as the previous phrase except for the word "there" is replaced with "here." Because of this phrase, it's more common to find dreidels with pe inscribed on them rather than shin. However, those in the Haredi communities say shin is the right letter for the Holy Land, as "there" refers to the Holy Temple itself. The dreidel is the game traditionally played during Hanukkah.

The Torah

Judaism is founded on the Torah, which represents the rabbinical teachings and law you're meant to follow as a Jew. Moses received the Torah from God himself to share with the people on Mount Sinai, and this collection of five books is considered one of Judaism's holiest items. A Torah scribe or Sefer writes the scroll using a certain parchment paper, which is then put into the ark (the Aron ha Kodesh), a sacred storage space. Writing the scrolls can take a year and a half to finish, as this involves preparing the animal skins to be used, as well as writing the scroll without making any mistakes. Mistakes make the scroll invalid or *pasul*. When the scroll is complete, it's called a Sefer Torah.

The Sefer Torah is a sacred scroll not just because it's the core of Judaism but because if you accidentally drop it in the synagogue, everyone present would have no choice but to fast for 40 days. Whenever the Jewish people had trouble and persecution, much effort would go into keeping the scrolls safe from harm because the Torah matters that much to them.

Every week, Jewish people gather to read the Torah as part of the activities during Shabbat services. These are the five alternative names for each book of the Torah, also called the Chameesha Choomshey Torah:

- Bresheit (Genesis)
- Shemot (Exodus)
- Vayicra (Leviticus)
- Bamidbar (Numbers)
- Devarim (Deuteronomy)

Moses received the Torah precisely 50 days after the Jews had left Egypt. The Torah describes the way God wants his people to live and express themselves, and it has 613 commandments for the people to follow. Ten of those are known as the Ten Commandments. These commandments are all written in Hebrew, the oldest Jewish language. The books are also known as the Law of Moses or Torat Moshe.

The entire scroll of the Torah is read in order over an entire year, starting from the end of the autumn celebration known as Sukkot. The aspects of the Torah that are read are known as the parshioth. There are usually anywhere from three to five chapters. Reading from the scroll is no mean feat because you need to be able to read the letters without needing the matching vowels. This means you've got to know the portion you're reading so well that you make no mistakes. The reading is more in the form of a song, and the tune it's sung to is rather ancient.

The scrolls are unfurled and set on a raised platform in the synagogue's center. This platform is known as the Bimah. No one touches the scrolls directly, as they use a pointer called a Yad instead. The Yad resembles a hand with a finger pointing out. The chanting must be done by someone trained specifically for this purpose, but the rabbi could also do it instead. If you're ever asked to join the congregation or witness a Shabbat reading, you should appreciate it because it's no mean thing. You're going to take part in an Aliyah, which is a word that means "going up."

The Tallit

When you're saying prayers, you'll have to use the tallit, which is a special prayer shawl. The shawl often has four corners, and it covers your shoulders. According to the Torah, all Jews have to do mitzvahs wearing a tallit with tzitzit, which are the knotted fringes on each corner of the shawl. The fringes, while beautiful, are more than just for aesthetic purposes. They are a reminder about the necessity of following the word of God, making no exemptions in the process. The cloth part is known as the begged, often made from cotton or wool and, now and then, from silk. Before putting the tallit on, you must say a certain blessing first. Some Jewish communities do not allow anyone to put it on unless or until it's their Bat or Bar Mitzvah. Other communities only whip out the tallit during the marriage.

The Tallit.

https://www.pexels.com/photo/a-person-in-a-tallit-reading-a-chumash-5974346/

There's no specific commandment in the Bible about having to put on a Tallit because the assumption during those times was that the people would have some sort of garment on to keep themselves covered anyway. The instruction given to the Israelites was that they had to attach the tzitzit to the corners of their garments, as indicated in Deuteronomy Chapter 22, verse 12.

The Kippah or Yarmulke

The Kippah.

https://www.pexels.com/photo/boy-lighting-menorah-3730985/

The Yarmulke is a small head covering that's round. It's worn by the Jews. The word Yarmulke is Yiddish, while Kippah is Hebrew. The purpose of this small hat is to remind the practitioner that no matter what, there's always someone who stands above you. The males of the Orthodox Judaism community always have their Kippah on, no matter what. Who wears a yarmulke, and when? Some Jewish sects will put them on only during religious ceremonies and services. Traditionally, all women are expected to keep their heads covered, particularly with the non-Orthodox Jewish denominations. You can expect the yarmulke to be offered as a gift during Bar and Bat Mitzvah occasions, and the recipient is expected to keep it on the entire time.

The Siddur

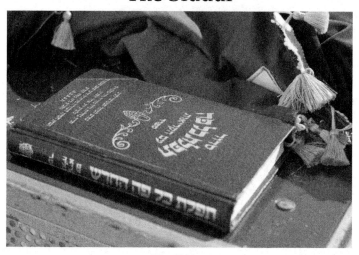

The Siddur.

The Siddur is a Jewish prayer book that contains Jewish liturgical texts. Siddur is "order" in Hebrew. The foundation of Siddur is the Prophets' prayers and the Torah. Note that not every prayer in the Siddur was there from the first versions, as some newer ones were incorporated over time. You may find all sorts of versions of Siddur, with some having prayers specifically for synagogue services held during the week, while others have prayers that cover Shabbat as well. You can also find Sukkot, Shavuot, and Passover prayers in the Siddur, which differs from one denomination to another.

The Mezuzah

The Mezuzah.

The mezuzah is kept at the doorpost. You can find the roots of the mezuzah in the Book of Deuteronomy, specifically in the portion where God told the Israelites they had to ensure they lived by his commandments and never forgot anything he told them. How? They were expected to write God's words on the doorposts of their homes. This special case has a scroll in it that has the words of Shema, and the outside of the container has Shin etched into it. If you're going to hang it up in your home, do so at an angle, and keep in mind you're not to allow people to fiddle with it because it's not just something for decoration but is a sacred object to be respected.

The Yad

The Yad.

The Yad tends to be used just as decoration, but when it's functional, it serves as a pointer. Rather than use your hand to read the Torah, you use the Yad instead so you can hold your place as the Torah is read in the synagogue or as it's sung. The Yad acts as your hand, and small wonder it does, since the word itself means "hand." It helps you to keep your place without soiling the Torah with your bare hands.

The Challah

The Challah.

This is a special kind of bread that Jewish people eat. It is golden brown, and the dough is twisted. This bread goes back to when the Israelites left Egypt and wandered about in the desert for 40 years. According to the Torah, the manna fell from the sky as they journeyed. This manna was like bread, and it helped sustain the Israelites. Now, Jews practice baking the challah, a sweet bread made with yeast and eggs and braided to form different shapes. Some bakers put a modern spin on things by adding chocolate chips or raisins. It's a lovely loaf to have but also of deep spiritual importance. During Rosh Hashanah, expect to be served challah that is round, but don't just eat it without knowing its significance. The circular shape is a reminder that life is a circle and a cycle. You might notice your challah loaf has 12 bumps on it. This is no coincidence, as each one represents an Israelite tribe. Here they are in order of birth:

- Reuben
- Simeon
- Levi
- Judah
- Issachar
- Zebulun
- Dan
- Naphtali
- Gad
- Asher
- Benjamin
- Joseph

Pomegranate

Pomegranate is a delicious fruit that has deep meaning in Judaism. It's meant to act as a reminder of the idea of love and the blessings of God that cause his people to be fertile in all their ways. Reading through the Book of Solomon, also known as the Song of Songs, you'll find the pomegranate makes frequent appearances. You should also know that even the seeds of this fruit are important, as they are a representation of the mitzvot which you must follow. Each of the 613 seeds in a pomegranate represents the mitzvot's 613 commandments. On Rosh Hashanah, this fruit is often served to make the new year one that is prosperous and wonderful for one and all.

The Shofar

The Shofar.
Jonathunder, CC BY-SA 3.0 <https://creativecommons.org/licenses/by-sa/3.0>, via Wikimedia Commons https://commons.wikimedia.org/wiki/File:ShofarSound.JPG

The shofar is a unique item. This is no ordinary horn, as there are specific times and events during which it is blown. If it's not Rosh Hashanah or Yom Kippur, don't expect to hear the shofar. Another time when it's often blown is in Elui, a Jewish month. The mitzvah commands that you must listen to the blast of the shofar during these specific times, and not only that, the shofar is meant to blast the teruah, shevarim, and tekiah. You can get this horn in all sizes and shapes, and children and adults are welcome to blast them as they like.

The Kiddush Cup

The Kiddush Cup.
Ivorymammoth at the English Wikipedia, CC BY-SA 3.0 <http://creativecommons.org/licenses/by-sa/3.0/>, via Wikimedia Commons https://commons.wikimedia.org/wiki/File:Kiddush_cup_jerusalem.jpg

This is a beautiful goblet made of silver, used for sacred drinks. This is one of the more common symbols in Judaism, and the word Kiddush translates to "sanctification." During the Passover seder or at a table specially prepared for Shabbat, you can expect to see the Kiddush make an appearance. It's used to bless the drink it carries, and when Shabbat officially comes to an end, you'll observe the standard practice is to begin Havdalah. Don't be too shocked if you notice someone continues to pour wine or grape juice into the Kiddush despite the fact that it's already flowing over. That's meant to represent the way God blesses his people, richly and abundantly, with no limit. This practice is a sign and a reminder that blessings are abundant for the coming week. This cup is also presented to a Bat or Bar Mitzvah as a gift.

Tefillin

Tefflin.
Yoavlemmer, CC BY-SA 4.0 <https://creativecommons.org/licenses/by-sa/4.0>, via Wikimedia Commons https://commons.wikimedia.org/wiki/File:IDF_soldier_put_on_tefillin.jpg

These are two black boxes made of leather. They are small and are usually bound to your forehead and just above your bicep. The Torah does not mention the tefillin, but the practice of placing the word of God on your arm and between both eyes is something the Torah talks about at least four times twice when the Israelites had to flee Egypt to go to the land promised to them by God, and twice more in the sacred Shema. You'll have these items bound to your arm and head, strapped securely in place, often with leather. It's standard practice to lay out the Tefillin when you pray early in the morning during the week, as this is what God wants.

The Chai

Chai is Hebrew for "life," and it's worn as an adornment on your neck. The word has the letters Chet and Yud. Chet happens to be the 8th Hebrew letter, and Yid is the 10th. Putting them together means you get the numerological value of 18, which is why the number 18 matters deeply in Judaism. Giving money to a Bat or Bar Mitzvah, a wedding, or even to charity is a practice to give in multiples of 18, as this represents the idea of giving life itself.

The Grogger

Every Jew knows the importance of recounting the story of Haman, who was an evil character in the Bible that was bent on the eradication of the Jews, much like several other people have been in Jewish history. When recounting this story, it's important to have the grogger present. The retelling is done during Purim, and it's important because it helps you remember how close Jews came to being annihilated and how God stepped in to save the people from Haman. You're obligated by law to hear the Purim story, which is what the Megillah is centered on. Each time Haman's name comes up, you take your grogger and give it a spin while booing him. The sound is reminiscent of grinding metal.

The Ten Commandments

All Jewish law is founded upon the ten commandments. They are depicted as large stone tablets with the commandments carved on them. They are commandments for how people should relate with God and how they should relate with other humans. The commandment that asks the faithful to honor their father and more is the connection between both relationships. There's a holiday known as the Shavuot, which happens in Spring. This holiday is meant to honor the receiving of the ten commandments by the Jewish people.

The Hamsa

The Hamsa.
Bluewind, CC BY-SA 3.0 <https://creativecommons.org/licenses/by-sa/3.0>, via Wikimedia Commons https://commons.wikimedia.org/wiki/File:Collection_of_khamsa.jpg

This symbol resembles a palm and is used not just by the Jews but by other religions as well. Usually worn as an amulet, you can put it on to keep yourself from becoming a victim of the evil eye. Hamsa is God's hand, shielding you from the deluge of your enemies and their ill intentions and machinations toward you, and that is why many Jews put on this amulet. Some people only think of it as a fashion piece, but they are missing out on its power by staying ignorant of what it's really about and how it can help them.

The Lulav and Etrog

A common Sukkot practice is to get four plants, myrtle, palm, willow, and etrog, and string them up together. These four plants then form something called the lulav. They wave this lulav in all directions to represent the idea that the Jewish people are one and to remind themselves of God's omnipresence. The standard practice is to shake the lulav while holding the etrog, and you must do this with deep reverence. When you want to buy the etrog, note that it's got to be in a velvet box. This way, the fruit (which is like a lemon) stays kosher, and the stem isn't destroyed.

The Magen David

The Magen David is also known as the Star of David and has six points. You may have seen this symbol on Israel's flag as a blue star against a white area, with blue frames surrounding the star. The symbol is said to be from the 1600s, and the Jewish people in Prague were the first to use the Magen David as their official symbol. After that, the symbol became popular all through Eastern Europe. By 1897, those who would go on to found Israel decided the Magen David would be the representation of Zionism, and this happened at the First Zionist Congress.

The Ketubah

The Ketubah must be signed by spouses who intend to get married to each other. It's a Jewish contract that regulates marriage based on Jewish law. Those who are to be wed must sign the contract first, and there have to be others present to act as witnesses to the process. You cannot get this signed if there isn't a rabbit to officiate and validate the document, which is a unique one, to say the least. Rather than a boring legal document, this one talks about the hopes and dreams of the happy couple through stunning artwork. The art could be done through any medium, from watercolor to oils and so on. Usually, the focal point of the art is the couple's home.

The Tree of Life

This is also known as Etz Chaim in Hebrew. It's meant to act as a metaphor, representing the Torah. The meaning of this symbol goes far back to the time of Eden when God created a garden full of wonderful trees. Among those trees were the tree of knowledge of good and evil and the tree of life. You'll find the Etz Chaim in most Jewish buildings and art, and many synagogues will work with the tree into their designs.

The Havdalah Set

Havdalah is a ritual meant to act as a separator between Shabbat and the other ceremonies of the week. The Shabbat has to be ended properly; a special day of rest held each week. Havdalah is that ending. During Havdalah, the Jews will say blessings over a cup full of wine, lovely-smelling spices, and a flame. Before the blessing, there has to be a clear sky at night so that three specific stars are visible to one and all. There are certain items required for you to celebrate the event of Havdalah, among them being a special tray, a braided candle, a box of spices, and the silver Kiddush. Everyone huddles together in the dark, forming a circle, and then blessings are sung while people pass the spices around to smell them. The spices are usually cloves, cinnamon, and cardamom. The wine from the Kiddush is poured over the candle's flame, marking the end of Shabbat.

Candles

Candles are a part of most Jewish rituals and holidays. When performing Shabbat, blessings are recited over candles. Traditionally, it's the matriarch who gets to light candles for Shabbat. When she's done, she must wave her hands around the flames thrice, working with a circular motion. This wave isn't random but is meant to bless the fires as they burn. These days, anyone other than the female head of the home can do this. If you could peek in on a Jewish family, you'll notice they have two candles meant to stand in for Shabbat's two obligations. These candles are intricately designed, and they stay in the family for generations. Sometimes they could be made of silver or clay.

The Seder Plate

Usually, these plates have separate parts for each item needed for the seder. The items are:

- **Parsley dipped in salt water:** This is a symbol of how much the people wept during their time with the Egyptians as their slave masters.

- **Charoset:** This is meant to be a representation of the mortar that the Israelites had to work with day in and day out while making bricks to build the Egyptian empire.

- **Horseradish or other bitter herbs:** This reminds the people of how terrible it was to be enslaved, to have one's free will taken from them, and be forced into a cruel, bitter life.

- **Lettuce or other greens:** This is yet another representation of the brutality of the enslaved way of living and how it completely breaks the soul.

- **A shank bone:** This is the sacrifice of the Israelites.

- **A roasted egg:** This represents the cycles of life and death.

The larger the feast, the more seder plates will be made available for every attendant to look upon and remember what their ancestors had to go through at the hands of their oppressors.

Chapter 3: The Sefirot and Ein Sof

The Sefirot are important aspects of the Kabbalah and represent the ten emanations through which the Ein Sof (or God) reveals his mysteries. Before diving into the Ein Sof and the Sefirot, here's a little more about the Kabbalah.

Kabbalah

When one lives by the Kabbalah, they are known as a Mekubbal. The Kabbalah's entire purpose is to make clear the connection between Ein Sof and his creation, making up the basis of Judaism, its beliefs, and practices. At first, the Jewish Kabbalists passed on their sacred texts within Judaism and would turn to the scriptures to shed light on the mystical knowledge they sought.

For traditional Kabbalists, the origins of the Kabbalah are from before the other religions in the world were a thing. They believe that the Kabbalah is the foundation of the politics, arts, sciences, religions, and world views that exist right now. Kabbalah comes from the earliest days of Jewish mysticism, and reinterpretations began during the 16th century in Ottoman Palestine. The Zohar is also important to the Kabbalah, which draws most of its meaning from there. Those who follow Kabbalah believe that studying this path and the Torah is important.

These are the foundational views of the Kabbalah:

1. There are ten aspects of God, and it is through these aspects that everything in life was created.

2. The Kabbalah's light of wisdom was given to the angels and Adam, Abraham, and Moses.

3. The human soul exists and has always existed before incarnating on Earth.

4. The soul reincarnates.

5. There are higher realms of existence or consciousness.

6. There are multiple universes.

7. Consciousness is connected at every level, from angels and demons to thought forms and incarnations.

8. Michael, Gabriel, Raphael, and Uriel are the four archangels, and they play powerful roles in the faith. Then there's Sandalphon, who, like Michael, is an angel of prayer. There's also Liliel, the Angel of the Night, and Lilith, the female devil.

9. Two Messiahs exist. One is of Joseph's bloodline, and the other is of David's.

10. Adam and Eve fell from grace because they couldn't make a correction that would move existence to a higher level of consciousness.

11. You can directly experience God and don't need to have Jesus or anyone else mediate on your behalf.

The Sefirot

The Tree of Life.

The Tree of Life is central to the Kabbalah. It's a sacred symbol that shows the ten Sephirot or Sefirot, which are the different aspects or revelations of the Creator. It's a spiritual light that shows the true nature of the Ein Sof. The singular form of the Sefirot is Sefirah or Sephirah. All ten of these aspects have the laws that govern all creation, including the things which were, are, and will be. The Tree of Life in Kabbalah is a model for all creation and man. The Tree of Life grows outwards from the Creator's divinity (Ein Sof, who has no end), being beyond the Sefirot themselves, as well as physical existence (that which comes from and is subordinate to the Sefirot). These are the ten Sefirot. It's important to note that they can be spelled differently:

- Keter or Kether(Crown)
- Hochmah or Chochmah(Wisdom)
- Binah (Understanding)
- Gevurah or Gewurah(Judgment)
- Hesed or Chesed(Kindness)
- Tiphereth (Beauty)
- Hod (Splendor)
- Netzah or Nezach(Eternity)
- Yesod or Jesod (Foundation)
- Malkhut or Malchuth (Kingdom)

Keter is the divine will of Ein Sof, the Creator, and the Sefirah, above all the others on the Kabbalistic Tree of Life. Just as the crown goes on the head, encircling it, the Keter contains all the other Sefirot. This Sefirah sits in a position that can't easily be unpacked and understood by the human mind, and for this reason, it's also known as "the most hidden of all hidden things." Alternatively, you may hear it referred to as Ayin, which means "nothing." Ayin represents the idea that the crown's secrets are so buried in mysteries that no one could try to deduce its true meaning or understand it through contemplation, debate, or any other means. Keter is the embodiment of compassion as well, as the Creator is the perfection in its final form, and Keter, being close to the Creator, has no flaws.

Hochmah is also known as Chochmah. It is the epitome of wisdom. This Sefirah is the Supernal Mind and the Oneness of all things. It's God's first act of creation, the beginning from which all things sprung. In the Kabbalah, wisdom is no ordinary thing. The undifferentiated mind isn't yet broken down by the thinking process. Consider it the first brilliant flash of an idea, whole and indivisible, before you begin breaking it down into its components, other ideas, and concepts. It is inspiration beyond division, where everything exists as one thing, which is the attribute of life not confined by space, time, or definitions. It's the unmanifested potential of all life.

Binah is understanding. Where Chochmah is undifferentiated inspiration, Binah is the separation of that mind or inspiration. It is the breakdown of the One into its many details, making it comprehensible for one and all. This is the level where ideas can exist on their own, on a level that makes it easy for anyone to examine them. This Sefirah is where everyone's soul comes from, and it is all about breaking things down into individual, distinct components. Binah is, therefore, the process of fleshing out the abstract into something more concrete.

Da'at is knowledge. This isn't exactly a Sefirah, but it serves as the connection between Chochmah (wisdom) and Binah (understanding). However, since it plays a very important role in this way, it acts like a legit Sefirah. This is why some systems like the Arizal will include Da'at in the Keter's place as the tenth Sefirah. Da'at is the invisible space between the Sefirot, and for Keter's energy to flow down to the other Sefirot, this space has to be crossed. Consider the process of creating something. At the start of the creation process, there's a crucial step: formulation of an idea. However, there's a chance that there's no will to flesh out that idea, or the will won't be enough to see the idea through to completion. Da'at is, therefore, like the will required to bring things that start to a finish, and you can think of it as an eleventh Sefirah, albeit hidden and parallel to Tiferet.

Hesed is also known as Chesed and is Kindness. It refers to the process of expansion and the concept of benevolence with no limits regarding God. God's benevolence is beyond benevolent, being the essence of abundance. It's about the divine quality of God that continues to expand without bounds. All souls can recognize this abundance, and they desire to be open to all things created, so they can express their goodness to it in the same way God expresses goodness to one and all.

Gevurah represents judgment, law, strength, and the limits of expansion. While Chesed represents expansion, Gevurah is contraction. Chesed allows energy to flow freely, while Gevurah acts as a means to limit and control the flow, acting as a counterbalance to Chesed. Both of these

Sefirot are balanced out by the Tiferet. Gevurah is the expression of restraint, discernment, and judgment. The reason Gevurah is necessary is that there has to be justice in the way that Chesed is shared among all. The universe operates on a merit system; therefore, you get the kindness you deserve. Gevurah is also essential for encouraging progress, action, and purpose. Its power and force are the requirements you must have to act on your desire for expansion, despite the obstacles you may encounter in the process.

Tiferet is also known as Tiphareth or Tiferet. The Sefirah lies in the middle of the Tree of Life and embodies the essence of truth and beauty. Tiferet acts as a balancing force for the entire Tree of Life, as, other than Malkhut, each Sefirah must flow into Tiferet. It represents the connection between heaven and Earth, which is depicted by the straight line that leads from Keter to Malchut. This Sefirah is on the Tree's middle column, which gives the other aspects balance, harmony in their functions, and a seamless synthesis of Chesed's outflow and Gevurah's restriction. You'll notice that the Tiferet is somewhat closer to Chesed. This proximity is why the Tiferet is known as Rachamim, compassion or mercy. It's also the aspect that is known for beauty, especially in the way it balances all the Sefirot.

Netzah is also called Netzach, and the Sefirah represents the concept of endless cycles and eternity. It also represents victory. This one is an extension of the power of Chesed. Netzach is the power that overcomes all obstacles in the way of the benevolence of God flowing to those meant to receive it. This is eternity itself, meaning that there are cycles that repeat endlessly, and they have no choice but to continue to keep all of creation in balance and stability.

Hod is the extension of Gevurah, representing the ideas of splendor and glory. This Sefirah is all about responsiveness. Where Netzach is all about the outpouring of all that is good, Hod is there to keep that benevolence in check. This way, it's impossible for God's benevolence to reach those who do not deserve it, and as a result, God continues to reign in his splendor and glory.

Yesod is the foundation. It acts as the connection between He who gives and they who receive. It is the unity between all other Sefirot and Malkhut. Yesod receives light from all the other Sefirot, synthesizes the light, and channels it as needed. This way, the emanations of the other aspects can flow to that which is created.

Malchut is also called Malkhut. It represents the Kingdom of the Divine and is why the physical world exists. This last Sefirah is distinct from the others because it doesn't have its own light. Instead, Malkhut receives light from the other aspects of the Tree of Life. Think of it like the moon, which only reflects sunlight and has no light of its own. Malkhut is the Sefirah that brings all things into existence in this lower, physical realm. Everything that has ever been is contained in this aspect, and its energy is dense and constricted. The world you can see around you is connected to Malkhut, representing the mouth and the power of the divine word of God. Malkhut also steadily interacts with Binah, as that which is abstract is made concrete in this created, physical world.

The Concept of Oneness

When you think of the Sefirot of the Tree of Life in Kabbalah, you should think of them as lights for your spiritual path. They are also responsible for all manifestations, showing the different aspects of Ein Sof. It's the same way a person can have different qualities, like loyalty, bravery, etc. Remember that the different Sefirot are not different gods, as only one God exists. They are simply different aspects of the same Creator, and one must never assume that there's duality in him.

The Oneness of the Divine is at the heart of Kabbalah. All followers must keep this in mind regardless of the circumstances. The Creator has no limits, which may be hard to comprehend from a limited human point of view. So the best thing we have are the Sephirot, which helps us to understand the limited aspects of the unlimited God.

Three Pillars, One Tree

Note that the Tree of Life has three pillars on the right, left, and middle. The pillar on the right represents expansion, the one on the left is constriction, and the middle acts as a balance between the other two pillars. These lines are meant to act as pillars of the faith working together as a synergistic whole. The pillars are Kindness (necessary as a reward for living righteously), Judgment (required to ensure balance and restitution to those who have been wronged or those who should get their just deserts for their choices), and Mercy (which makes it possible for one and all to be forgiven and brought back into the loving grace of Ein Sof). The right pillar is masculine, all about action. It is the giver. There's also the pillar on the left, which is more about receiving and being passive, both of which are feminine qualities. Finally, the pillar in the middle connects the other two and brings balance to these energies so that they manifest as they should.

Sephirothic Correspondences

The correspondences of the Sefirot refer to symbols, qualities, and other associations that can help you understand what each Sefirah stands for. Below are the correspondences of the Sefirot. Note that some of the planets here aren't actual planets. The element refers to the physical, classical elements that match the Sefirah's nature. Also, there's the Briatic correspondence, an abstract quality that captures the essence of the Sefirah's expression. The illusion refers to how the Sefirah's energy can cause us not to judge things clearly, showing up as "obvious truths," while the obligation is what you need to express at that level. Virtue and Vice are the Sefirah's energy manifesting for better or worse in your personality. You'll also see the corresponding Qliphoth (more on that later), spiritual experience, the name of God used to invoke the Sefirah's power, and more.

Keter

Meaning: Crown

Color: Pure white

Number: 1

Spiritual Experience: Union with God

Archangel: Metatron

Angel Order: Chaioth ha Qadesh

Name of God: Eheieh

Qliphoth: Futility

Planet: Rashith ha Gilgalim

Briatic Correspondence: Unity

Illusion: Attainment

Virtue: Attainment

Vice: Nil

Alternative Names: the Greater Countenance (Macroprosopus), the Smooth Point, Concealed of the Concealed, Rum Maalah, the Highest Point, Existence of Existences, Ancient of Days

Keywords: God, unity, pure consciousness, union, the Godhead, emanation, source, manifestation.

Chokhmah

Meaning: Wisdom

Color: Gray, silver, or white

Number: 2

Spiritual Experience: Face-to-face vision of God

Archangel: Raziel

Angel Order: Auphanim

Name of God: Jah

Qliphoth: Arbitrariness

Planet: Mazlot

Briatic Correspondence: Revolution

Illusion: Independence

Virtue: Good

Vice: Evil

Alternative Names: The Supernal Father, Abba, the Father.

Keywords: The wellspring, lifeforce, pure creative energy

Binah

Meaning: Understanding

Color: Black

Number: 3

Spiritual Experience: Vision of Sorrow

Archangel: Cassiel

Angel Order: Aralim

Name of God: Elohim

Qliphoth: Fatalism

Planet: Shabbathai (or Saturn)

Briatic Correspondence: Comprehension

Illusion: Death

Virtue: Silence

Vice: Inertia

Alternative Names: Ama, Marah, Aima, Khorsia, the Throne, the Crone, the Mother, the Superior Mother, the Mother of Form, Intelligence, the Fifty Gates of Understanding.

Keywords: Constraint, slowness, limits, karma, infertility, old age, time, fate, the womb and gestation, natural law, space, death, weaving and spinning, fertility, containment, boundedness, annihilation, enclosure, mother.

Chesed

Meaning: Mercy

Color: Blue

Number: 4

Spiritual Experience: Vision of Love

Archangel: Zadkiel

Angel Order: Chasmalim

Name of God: El

Qliphoth: Ideology

Planet: Tzadekh (or Jupiter)

Briatic Correspondence: Authority

Illusion: Self-righteousness (or being right)

Virtue: Humility

Vice: Gluttony, hypocrisy, bigotry, tyranny

Obligation: Humility, obedience

Alternative Names: Majesty, love, magnificence, Gedulah.

Keywords: Secular power, spiritual power, creativity, vision, inspiration, authority, leadership, submission, waste, excess, the atom bomb, service, birth, obliteration, the Annihilation Myth.

Gevurah

Meaning: Strength

Color: Red

Number: 5

Spiritual Experience: Vision of Power

Archangel: Camael

Angel Order: Seraphim

Name of God: Elohim Gevor

Qliphoth: Bureaucracy

Planet: Madim (or Mars)

Briatic Correspondence: Power

Illusion: Invincibility

Virtue: Energy, courage

Vice: Cruelty

Obligation: Loyalty, courage

Alternative Names: Justice, Din, fear, Pachad

Keywords: Cold retribution, executed law, power, cruelty, justice, domination, oppression, the Power Myth, catabolism, needed destruction, martial arts.

Tifereth

Meaning: Beauty

Color: Yellow

Number: 6

Element: Fire

Spiritual Experience: Vision of Harmony

Archangel: Michael

Angel Order: Malachim

Name of God: Aloah va Daath

Qliphoth: Hollowness

Planet: Shemesh (or the Sun)

Briatic Correspondence: Wholeness, centrality

Illusion: Identification

Virtue: Devotion to the Great Work

Vice: Self-importance, pride

Obligation: Integrity

Command: Dare

Alternative Names: The Microprosopus, the King, Melekh, the Son, Zoar Anpin, Rachamin, charity.

Keywords: Wholeness, balance, identity, integrity, self-importance, harmony, centrality, self-sacrifice, the Philosopher's Stone, the Self, the Son of God, the solar plexus, the Great Work, the King.

Netzach

Meaning: Firmness, victory

Color: Green

Number: 7

Element: Water

Spiritual Experience: Vision of Beauty Triumphant

Archangel: Haniel

Angel Order: Elohim

Name of God: Jehovah Tzabaoth

Qliphoth: Routine, habit

Planet: Nogah (or Venus)

Briatic Correspondence: Nurture

Illusion: Projection

Virtue: Unselfishness

Vice: Selfishness

Obligation: Responsibility

Command: Know

Keywords: Emotions, drives, sensual beauty, feelings, luxury, pleasure, passion, libido, nurture, ecstasy, sympathy, empathy.

Hod

Meaning: Splendor, glory

Color: Orange

Number: 8

Element: Air

Spiritual Experience: Vision of Splendor

Archangel: Raphael

Angel Order: Beni Elohim

Name of God: Elohim Tzabaoth

Qliphoth: Rigidity

Planet: Kokab (or Mercury)

Briatic Correspondence: Abstraction

Illusion: Order

Virtue: Truth, honesty

Vice: Dishonesty

Obligation: Learn

Command: Will

Keywords: Language, the sciences, communication, reason, logic, abstraction, conceptualization, the concept of money, speech, media communication, trickery, healing, medicine, writing, philosophy, protocol, pedantry, the abstract Kabbalah system, the Law, rights, theft, territory, ownership.

Yesod

Meaning: Foundation

Color: Purple

Number: 9

Element: Aethyr (or ether)

Spiritual Experience: Vision of the Machinery of the Universe

Archangel: Gabriel

Angel Order: Cherubim

Name of God: Shaddai el Chai

Qliphoth: Robotism, zombieism

Planet: Levanah (or the Moon)

Briatic Correspondence: Perception, receptivity

Illusion: Security

Virtue: Independence

Vice: Idleness

Obligation: Trust

Command: Go

Alternative Names: The Treasure House of Images

Keywords: Imagination, interface, appearance, perception, image, the noon, glamor, instinct, hidden infrastructure, the unconscious, dreams, illusion, divination, tides, things as they seem to be and not as they are in reality, crystals, mirrors, sex, reproduction, genitals, glue, tunnels, the astral realm, aethyr, cosmetics, secret doors, instinctive magic or psychism, shamanic tunnels.

Malkuth

Meaning: Kingdom

Color: Brown (or black, olive green, russet red, citrine)

Number: 10

Element: Earth

Spiritual Experience: Vision of the Holy Guardian Angel

Archangel: Sandalphon

Angel Order: Ishim

Name of God: Adonai Malekh, Adonai ha Aretz

Qliphoth: Stasis

Planet: Cholem Yesodeth (or Earth, the sphere of the elements, the Breaker of the Foundations)

Briatic Correspondence: Stability

Illusion: Materialism

Virtue: Discrimination

Vice: Inertia, avarice

Obligation: Discipline

Command: Silence

Alternative Names: The Inferior Mother, the Gate, the Queen, Malkah, the Gate of Tears, Kallah, the Bride, the Gate of Death, the Virgin.

Keywords: Mother Earth, the Earth, the natural world, the physical elements, physical matter, sticks and stones, possessions, incarnation, feces, inertia, stability, solidity, practicality, heaviness, death of the body.

On Ein Sof

Ein Sof is the Divine God. It is the Infinite God who has no humanly discernible form. Those who follow the Kabbalistic path understand that God and his creation continue to evolve together and are the embodiment of different qualities and stages. The later stages are not just opposed to the earlier ones but also encompass them. Ein Sof is equal parts as simple as complex a being. It is everything and nothing at the same time, the embodiment of what is revealed and that remains secret. Ein Sof contains and expresses illusion and reality, being a human creation and creating humans simultaneously. As Ein Sof continues to evolve and expand, what can be gleaned from its revelation is that it is nothing or Ayin, as well as the totality of existence and the Infinite Will called Ratzon. Ein Sof represents wisdom, thought, and all things considered valuable and important (expressed through the Sefirot).

Ein Sof is the unity of the masculine and the feminine. If you've followed so far, it embodies every possible contradiction. The nature of Ein Sof implies that it is always in the process of redefining and recreating itself. One way this recreation manifests itself is in human creativity, where everyone works with hands, minds, and spirits to save a world full of chaos and contradiction.

There are various terms that Kabbalists use to refer to the hidden God, like "the concealed light," "that which thought cannot contain," "the concealment of secrecy," and so on. These terms express clearly that Ein Sof cannot be known in full. However, there are other terms like "Great Reality," "Indifferent Unity," "Root of all roots," "Prime Mover," "Cause of Causes," and so on that make it clear that Ein Sof is where everything that exists begins, as well as the combination of all things. The Sefer Yetzirah says this about Ein Sof: "Restrain your mouth from speaking and your heart from thinking, and if your heart runs, let it return to its place."

If you've ever wondered why anything exists and what the purpose of humanity is, the answer lies in Ein Sof. Being the source of all value and meaning, known and unknown, Ein Sof created the world so he could understand himself. The values of Ein Sof were originally in abstract form, and the only way to know them was to have them made real or concrete in humanity. Ein Sof contains and is both being and nothingness, but Ein Sof cannot be complete unless and until he becomes real — a process that happens through mankind's spiritual activities. Ein Sof's reflection can be seen in the human heart, soul, and deeds. If you'd like to learn more about the Sefirot and Ein Sof, look at the Sefer Yetzirah and study it.

The Qliphoth

The Qliphoth are the polar opposite of the Sefirot. Also known as the Klippot (singular, Qliphah), they represent evil in the Kabbalah. The word Kippot is Hebrew for "peels." The reason they are known as peels is that they are nothing but empty husks that used to contain the spark of divinity, and they were cast down from heaven after Adam and Even had gone against the commandment of God to not eat of the Tree of Knowledge of Good and Evil in the Eden, as is recorded in Genesis. The Qliphoth can appear in different forms, from road accidents to natural disasters, demons, and other mythical creatures.

Just as there are ten emanations or enumerations of the Divine, there are ten Qliphoth manifestations or emanations of darkness. This darkness cannot receive the light of God. You may think of the Qliphoth as the attributes of a condition against God. They act as the answer to the age-old question, "If there's a God and he's all-powerful, how and why does evil exist?" It is believed that God is pure and divine and that his light shines into the darkness with the ten rays of the Sefirot. When God's light does shine in the darkness, it is said that new worlds are formed. The closer you decide to get to God, the more his light will shine in your world and the less evil you'll have to deal with. The Qliphoth are the epitome of chaos and darkness, which held sway until God formed the light. These are the emanations of darkness in their personality forms:

- Thaumiel (ruled by Satan and Moloch)
- Ghagiel (ruled by Beelzebuth)
- Sathariel (ruled by Lucifuge)

- Gamichicoth (ruled by Astaroth)
- Golachab (ruled by Asmodeus)
- Thagirion (ruled by Belfegor)
- Arab-Zaraq (ruled by Baal)
- Samael (ruled by Adramelech)
- Gamaliel (ruled by Lilith)
- Nahemoth (ruled by Naamah)

Chapter 4: The Power of the Name of God

Before getting into the power of the name of God, it's important to address the divinity of the Hebrew language. First, Hebrew is known as "the Holy Tongue," or Lashon Hakodesh. For one thing, no words in Hebrew can be used to describe semen, excreta, private parts, or sexual acts, as observed by Maimonides. The Hebrew language refers to these things through figures of speech. However, according to Nachmanides, it's the Holy tongue because this was the language chosen by God to reach out to his people through the prophets of old.

Hebrew is known as the Holy Tongue.
Dav!dB, CC BY-SA 3.0 <https://creativecommons.org/licenses/by-sa/3.0>, via Wikimedia Commons https://commons.wikimedia.org/wiki/File:Hebrew_Bible_Wordle_-%D7%A4%D7%95%D7%A1%D7%98%D7%A8_%D7%94%D7%AA%D7%A4%D7%9C%D7%92%D7%95%D7%AA_%D7%94%D7%9E%D7%9C%D7%99%D7%9D_%D7%91%D7%AA%D7%A0%22%D7%9A.png

Hebrew is a powerful language. The Torah makes it clear that before the occurrence at the Tower of Babel, everyone on Earth had the same language, and that language was Hebrew. Thanks to this language, those building the Tower of Babel could make it as far as they did to begin with. So, to keep them from building the tower until it reached heaven, God decided to scramble their languages, which is how the many languages we know today came to be.

Hebrew as the Language of Creation

The Book of Genesis discusses how God created the entire world. He said, "Let there be light," and there was light. Most people who read this passage assume that it is only rhetoric. However, the truth is that the words spoken by God have energy that *formed the light.* In the Torah, you will find ten phrases like the one he uttered described. These phrases are known as the Ten Utterances and are responsible for the world's creation. There isn't a single thing in existence that was not created with the power in those Hebrew words.

Those who practice the Kabbalah say that the word of God is not like regular human speech. When you speak common words, they are gone forever and accomplish nothing. However, the spoken word of God is everlasting. In the Book of Psalms, you will find a verse that says, "Forever, O God, your word stands in the heavens." This implies that God's Ten utterances are still at work in the heavens. Those utterances continue to give the world energy and vitality, recreating it as needed. Everything in existence is created through the power of words. Therefore, the Hebrew name of all objects carries the energy that sustains the existence of each one.

The Paradox

If you've followed so far, you may have noted a paradox. On the one hand, Maimonides says that excreta, semen, sexual organs, and acts don't have Hebrew words to describe them because they are vulgar. On the other hand, everything in the world exists thanks to the energy of its Hebrew name, which powers it. Therefore, shouldn't these so-called nasty things have Hebrew names too? Therefore, wouldn't that imply that the vulgar and profane are holy, as postulated by Nachmanides?

To figure out this conundrum, it is important to dive into Maimonides' musings about reality before sin and after sin. Before the sin of Adam and Eve, where they ate of the Tree of Knowledge of Good and Evil, sex and sexual organs were no more special than any other organs or human activities, and there must have been names for them in the Holy Hebrew language. However, after the fall of Adam and Eve, when they'd both become aware of the sensuality they had, these organs became connected to the sin of lust automatically. Therefore, there's no way to know their actual names since the concept of them being holy is beyond human understanding. However, both Nachmanides and Maimonides agreed on the fact that sexuality could either be profound or profane. It all comes down to context and intent.

To summarize the point about the holiness of the Hebrew language, Rabbi Yeshayah ha-Levi Horowitz (Shaloh) has said that when it comes to the alphabet and words of other languages, they are the creations of man. However, the Holy Tongue is special in that the name, sound, and even the shape of each letter of the Hebrew alphabet have spiritual characteristics and unique energies. So holy is Hebrew that the Zohar claims that speaking in the Holy Tongue causes the Divine Presence or Shechinah to rest on you. However, since the language is so holy, it is often only spoken when used to study or teach the Torah and to pray.

While learning how to *speak* in Hebrew for prayer, learning and studying are more important; it matters deeply that you understand the words coming out of your mouth. You need to understand the meaning of the words you *read*. This is why the Talmud is in Aramaic, and if you don't understand Hebrew properly, it's best to do your prayers in the language you know best.

The Names of God

Ein Sof happens to be just one of many names for the Creator. God's true, complete name is Shem HaM'phorash in Hebrew. Sometimes, it is written as Shem HaMephorash, Shem ha-Mehporash, or Schemhamphoras. This name means "the explicit name," and it was originally a Tannaitic description of God's hidden name in the Kabbalah and other more mainstream Jewish ideologies. This name has either 4, 12, 22, 42, or 72 letters. Sometimes the letters are written in triads.

Now, on to the versions of God's name with 12, 22, and 42 letters. Maimonides believed that Shem HaM'phorash was only used for the 4-letter name of God or the Tetragrammaton, which is either spelled JHVH or YHWH, pronounced as Jehovah or Yahweh. You'll find the 12-letter form of God's name in the Talmud, but it wasn't known to the Kabbalah and wasn't found in Jewish mysticism. The variant of God's name with 22 letters was first written in Sefer Raziel HaMalakh as Anaktam Pastam Paspasim Dionsim. The name's origins in this form aren't known, and there's no clear connection to Aramaic or Hebrew, at least none that has been found yet. There's also no way to conclude that its roots are Zoroastrian or Greek. However, Generic connections suggest the name predates the Sefer Raziel itself.

Hai Gaon described a 42-letter form of God's name and said while the consonants of God's name are known to one and all, the actual pronunciation isn't. Some say the first part of the name is Abigtaz. Others as Abgitaz. Some call the last part Shekuzit, while others call it Shakvazit. The different variations in the name could indicate that this version is rather ancient, so the Hebrew vowels have been lost over time. It comes from the first 42 letters in the Hebrew Bible and can also be found in the Sefer Raziel HaMalakh.

God's 72-Fold Name

Finally, there's the 72-fold name of God, which is of grave significance to Sefer Raziel HaMalakh. This name comes from the Book of Exodus, Chapter 14, verses 19 to 21. It is read boustrophedonically (from right to left and left to right) to give 72 names. Each of these names has only three letters. Rashi and the Sefer HaBahir from circa 1150 to 1200 explain how the method of getting these names works. According to the Kabbalah, the 72-fold name helped Moses cross the Red Sea, and it's said that this name can give holy men the power needed to perform miracles (like healing the six), casting out demons, stopping natural disasters, and killing enemies. It is also said that this sacred name can be used to create golems. As you've probably already figured, the point is that there's power in Hebrew letters and power in the names of God.

These 72 names aren't to be thought of as common names like Drew or Dave or Daisy, but they are 72 sequences of three Hebrew letters each that have the power to defy all the laws of nature and human nature. This was a formula written in code in the portion of the Bible describing the parting of the Red Sea. It's a secret no priest, Rabbi, or other Jewish mysticism scholar knew about. Only a few Kabbalists were aware of it, and they waited for the right time to share it with one another. You don't need to know how to speak Hebrew to enjoy the power of these names in your life. Each name acts as an index to certain spiritual energies or frequencies. Just looking at the letters or bringing them up in your imagination can connect you to those frequencies so that you can repair your soul as needed. Sometimes, the attribute "el" or "yah" can be added to the names to give you the names of the Geniis (the 72 Angels).

The shapes, sequences, sounds, and vibrations of each name have a light that purifies your heart and soul, eliminating the destructive flaws in your nature. The energy of these names is sacred and banishes anxiety, fear, and other detrimental emotions. So powerful are the Hebrew letters that the very word for letter in Hebrew means vibration or pulse, showing there is indeed a flow of energy when these words are spoken. The Hebrew alphabet is above and beyond geography, race, religion, and language. The three letters in each name can be thought of as having a positive charge, a negative charge, and a necessary ground wire to allow energy to flow. If you take advantage of the power in God's name, you should know the spiritual symbolism of each letter and number. A fantastic book on how to use God's names is The 72 Names of God: Technology for the Soul.

The Names of God

Just because God's names are too holy to be spoken in vain doesn't mean they should be lost from a lack of use to the sands of time. So it's essential to know them and know what they mean. God's names help everyone understand the different aspects of God and can help you with your magical practices. You should also study the spiritual symbolism of each letter to help you make the most of your prayers and practice using God's name. With that said, here are some of the names of God you can use in prayer and magic – and their meanings.

Yahweh: The one who has always existed and will keep on existing. The self-existent one needs nothing and no one to permit him to exist. This means you can lean on him whenever you need strength or someone to back you up.

Adonai: The King of kings and Lord of lords who reigns supremely. Therefore, calling on this name will force all authorities, principalities, and powers, causing you trouble to bow to the one and only God and do as you ask.

Yahweh Maccaddeshem: The Lord who sanctifies. This is the God who is able and willing to forgive all sin and to grant his Holy Spirit to you so that you can become as pure and loving as he is in all your ways.

Yahweh Rohi: The Lord who is your shepherd. You have no reason to want or lack anything. God takes care of you as a shepherd cares for their sheep. He keeps you from getting lost, hungry, thirsty, or having any unmet needs. This is the God who takes you to still, calm lakes, and gives you the fat of the land so you can experience abundant life. Use this name when you have needs you need to meet.

Yahweh Shammah: The ever-present Lord. He chooses to remain with you and won't forsake you. He is your best friend and confidant forever, and you can trust him not to betray you. This is excellent when you're on your own and need someone on your side.

Yahweh Rapha: The Lord, your healer. If you're ever going through health issues, whether mental, physical, emotional, or spiritual, you can call on God with this name to come to your aid.

Yahweh Tsidkenu: The Lord your righteousness. This name is excellent because it reveals the truth: You may be flawed, but through God, you can find yourself forgiven, purified, and perfect in his image.

Yahweh Jireh: The Lord is your provider. If you ever find yourself lacking or having needs that desperately need to be met, this is an excellent way to call on God for guaranteed assistance.

Yahweh Nissi: The Lord, your banner. This means you're not alone, no matter what you try to accomplish. You have backup from the Divine Creator himself. You will get victory in whatever you set out to do using this name, whether it's spiritual warfare or another challenge you face in the physical world. The Bible speaks of the Lord raising a banner of his love over you and covering you when the enemy wants to overwhelm you, much like a flood. Use this name when you want God to fight on your behalf.

Yahweh Shalom: The Lord, the peaceful one. Whenever you're dealing with strife or issues that have you constantly biting your nails in anxiety, that's the perfect time to call on Jehovah Shalom. He will act as the calm in the eye of the storm, keeping you sane while everything and everyone else falls apart. He will give you "the peace that passes all understanding," acting as your shield, strength, and shelter.

Yahweh Sabbaoth: He is the God in charge of the hosts of angels beyond numbering. These angels are mighty, destroying hell's armies with ease, as well as those who would attempt to mess with God's anointed one (that's you). You can call on Jehovah Sabbaoth when you need divine firepower to help you get through enemies' attacks.

Yahweh Ghmolah: The Lord of recompense. God's word says, "Vengeance is mine. I will repay." When you've been wronged, willfully hurt by someone, or mistreated, you don't have to waste your energy or time going after them. Call on Jehovah Ghmolah to come to your defense, and watch as the other person pays for everything they've done to you. Stand still and watch God restore everything you lost.

Elohim: The almighty and powerful Creator. He is the Lord of all, he who is above all others. He has power and might be beyond anything you could ever imagine. When you're dealing with a situation or a person that has you feeling completely defeated, call on Elohim.

El Elyon: The Highest God. Is there something or someone in your life that you find intimidating? Don't despair. Call on El Elyon, and every knee must bow before him on your behalf. No one is higher or greater than him, and all must acknowledge his authority. Exercise his divine power by using this name.

El Gibhor: This is the God of Might who can save one and all. It doesn't matter what you're dealing with. There's power in this name to help you overcome it all.

El Olam: The Lord the everlasting. All else is temporary, but he lasts forever. Your struggles, obstacles, and problems are temporary. God outlasts them all, and so does his love for you. The promises he has made you are everlasting as well. When you feel yourself losing faith because of whatever you're facing at the moment, don't despair. Use this name to remind yourself that God wins every time and is not about to stop winning on your behalf.

El Roi: The Strong One who sees all. Sometimes, you may feel like no one knows what you're going through or that no one actually sees you. Know that he does. He is with you and knows you even better than you know yourself. He knows your heart's desire, and because of his infinite love for you, he will do all he can to bring you to a good place. Trust him.

El Shaddai Rohi: The Lord, the one true God. Use this name when someone in your life has set themselves up in a position of power to torment you. It will serve as a reminder that you answer to no one but the Creator, who will surely put that person in their place. You can also use this name to address situations that have taken up so much of your time, energy, and resources.

El Chuwl: The Lord who gave birth. God is your Father. He knew you and loved you before you were born. The Creator has plans for you, and even if at the moment you may not be able to see them clearly, or it may feel like you're on your own, you're not. Trust him, and he'll make your life beautiful.

El Deah: Call this name when you need wisdom, knowledge, and understanding. It means "God of Knowledge." Attempting to be wise on your own will never work. You must reach out to God and learn from him by keeping his commandments. You should also listen to the messages he has for you and trust what he says.

Attiyq Youm: God, the Ancient of Days. He is eternal and has existed before, which means he has all power and authority over everyone and everything. Invoke God's power with this name when you need to get results that aren't forthcoming because of difficult people or situations.

Chapter 5: Angels and Their Hierarchy

Angels in Judaism are known as the Mal'akim (single form, mal'ak). It means "messenger." These angels are supernatural beings, and you can find mention of them in the Tanakh (the Hebrew Bible), writings from different rabbis, pseudepigrapha (falsely attributed texts), and apocrypha. These angels have different hierarchies; according to the Talmud, their energy is fire.

According to the Tanakh, each Patriarch of the Jewish faith had angels appear to them. Hagar, Lot, Abraham, Joshua, Moses, and others had witnessed angels. They went up and down Jacob's ladder in the Book of Genesis and showed themselves to Jacob. An angel also got in Balaam's way in the Book of Numbers. Isaiah the prophet talked about the angel of presence, also called the mal'ak panav, in the Book of Isaiah; in this book, Isaiah spoke about how he saved God's people. The Book of Psalms also discusses how God assigns angels to care for his people.

The Origin of Angels

The angel of the Lord has been perceived by generation after generation, yet the image of this being is not easily deduced. In the Tanakh, the angel tends to show up in a certain way: First, there's a narrative introduction of this being. The Angel of the Lord is usually portrayed as a deity in certain books of the Bible, such as when he assured fertility in Genesis, Chapter

21, verse 18. Another instance of the being acting as a deity is in the Second Book of Kings, Chapter 19, verses 32 to 26, where he demonstrated his might by wiping out an army with a single blow. Then there are times when the being speaks as though he were the one true God, like in chapter 3 of Exodus, verses 2, to 4. Then those who interact with this angel tend to act reverently toward the being as if they were a deity. This causes one to wonder if it was just an angel or God himself who showed up at those times.

Roles of Angels

They help with healing. There are instances in the Bible where the angels could heal people from impurity, but some wonder if the Seraphim would qualify as angels. For instance, Isaiah the prophet saw them praising God, and according to his account, they had such powerful voices that they caused the pivots on thresholds to rattle, and the whole temple was full of smoke. This is according to the Book of Isaiah, Chapter 6, verses 3 to 4. Their power was so intense that the prophet couldn't help but feel he wasn't worthy or clean enough to be in their presence, let alone witness their splendor. Then one of the Seraphim came to him and touched his mouth with a burning coal from the altar. Thanks to the angel, the prophet Isaiah discovered that he didn't have to worry about the things he'd done and said in the past. He had been forgiven, and all had been forgotten as soon as the burning coal came in contact with his lips. In the Book of Zechariah, Joseph had to be present before God and the being known as the angel of the Lord (Joshua 3:3). Also, when Zechariah had to be in their divine presence, it was clear to one and all that his clothes were in dire need of washing. So on the angel's command, Zechariah stripped and then put on the clothes that had been presented to him. The new set of clothes was clean, fit for all celebrations to come, but more than just being clean, they were a *metaphor*. The angel let Zechariah know that the process of changing out of the old clothes into the new ones meant that he no longer had to deal with the guilt and shame of his past, and therefore, you could see this as a true, healing miracle. How many souls are plagued by the wrongs they've done in the past? Imagine being able to move past all of that and start anew. This was the gift offered to Zechariah, and as he took it, so should you as a practicing Jew. The New Testament also talks about an angel that would come and trouble the waters at a certain fountain so whoever got in could be healed of whatever afflictions they had.

They help with prayer: In the Book of Zechariah, God lets Zechariah know that he's upset with his ancestors because of their terrible actions. He promised that if they were to come back to him, he would come back to them too. God's angel then decided to take it upon himself to advocate for the people God was so upset with. He said a prayer for them. In that prayer, he asked God to be clear about how long he felt it was okay to remain upset with and to continue punishing the people of Jerusalem and Judah because their relationship had taken hit after hit for seven decades, and it only made sense that God should eventually have mercy on them and make it possible to patch things up. Angels can pray on your behalf, too.

They go to war: Angels are not to be trifled with, as they are experts in matters of war. They are as fierce as they can be loving and understanding, and they are swift to uproot all evil machinations so that good can prevail. The Bible mentions four different visions of the end of the world, also known as the apocalypse, specifically in the Book of Daniel, which notes all the visions Daniel had. It talks about the battle between the Persian prince and Archangel Gabriel, who had informed Daniel there was no need to be alarmed since Archangel Michael was leading the charge against Persia and all would be well soon. So, Gabriel and Michael waged war against Persia for the sake of good. In Daniel Chapter 12, verse 1, Gabriel also says that Michael is responsible for protecting the Israelites from harm.

They pass on messages. Many passages from the Tanakh speak of angels acting as messengers. The truth is there's no actual Hebrew word that matches the English word "angel." These beings sometimes seem like regular humans, and usually, they are men. Unlike seraphim, they don't have wings. So it is important to note when a human messenger is being discussed in the Bible verses – and when it is an angelic messenger.

Despite all that, angels acting as messengers are vital because they serve as a connection between humanity and God and keep the needed space between the Creator and his creation. The angels carry heavenly, divine knowledge with them, and they can only share that knowledge with humans if God permits it and only if it is necessary to pass on a message. When an angel shares what God knows with those on Earth, that angel serves as God himself, and the angel's personal identity doesn't matter or exist in the process. The angel acts as God's very mouthpiece.

You can find many instances of angels serving as messengers in books of the Old Testament. Among them is the tale of the three mysterious men in the story of Sodom and Gomorrah (Genesis, Chapter 18, verse 1 to Chapter 19, verse 23). An angel also informed Samson's mother about the sort of baby she was to give birth to in the Book of Judges, Chapter 13, verses 3 to 5. The angels often had their identities disguised in these stories and were only about their job: Passing on a message.

Angels act as teachers: In the apocalyptic writings, there are stories about angels being teachers, especially in the Books of Daniel, Zechariah, and Ezra. Here, some people had the privilege of seeing prophetic visions (some terrifying, others mysterious). These people needed guidance to understand what they had just witnessed. So, the angel explained the visions so the prophet could grasp what they had seen, and they, in turn, could share more accurate knowledge about the end times with his people.

The angel's knowledge about the apocalypse had implications that affected both heaven and Earth and was very important to the Israelites, who were oppressed at the time and needed to understand why God was doing nothing about their situation. The angels embody heaven's might and God's authority, while they possess the warmth and love necessary to comfort the humans and remain relatable.

Hierarchies of Angels in Judaism

Rabbi Moshe ben Maimon, also known as Maimonides, talks about how there are 10 different hierarchies of angels, which he wrote about in Mishneh Torah around 1180. Here are the angelic rankings from the highest to the lowest. Note that other mystical texts may have different hierarchies, numbering more or less than 10. However, Maimonides' version is the most important one.

1. **Chayot ha Kodesh:** These angels are enlightened and responsible for upholding God's throne and ensuring the Earth remains in its rightful place in space. These angels emit powerful light, making them look like flames of fire. One of the famous angels in this ranking is the archangel Metatron. Metatron is in charge of the Chayot ha Kodesh, according to the Kabbalah, and it happens that he is the archangel of Keter.

2. **Ophanim:** The Ophanim never sleep. This is because they are responsible for keeping watch over God's throne. They are also an incredibly wise group of angels, and their name comes from the Hebrew word *ophan,* meaning "wheel." The Torah talks about them in the first chapter of Ezekiel, saying that their spirits are housed in wheels that they use to move wherever they want. Archangel Raziel is in charge of these angels and is connected to the Chokhmah Sefirah.

3. **Erelim:** The Erelim are among the bravest angels under the rulership of archangel Tzaphkiel. These beings also happen to be quite understanding. They are known as the valiant ones and tend to show up when a national tragedy is about to happen or when death is imminent.

4. **Hashmallim:** The Hashmallim are very graceful, kind, and loving. They are led by archangel Zadkiel, according to the Kabbalah. Zadkiel is the one who was mercifully kind in the Book of Genesis, Chapter 22 when Abraham was just about to sacrifice Isaac, his son. This angel is connected to the Chesed Sefirah.

5. **Seraphim:** The Seraphim are the ones who are all about justice. According to the Kabbalah, archangel Chamuel leads the Seraphim. The Torah talks about a vision of the prophet Isaiah, where he saw the Seraphim around God in heaven. The Seraphim are six-winged creatures with two wings over their faces, two wrapped around their feet, and two for flight. Chamuel is also *Camael,* who is in charge of the Gevurah Sefirah.

6. **The Malakhim:** these are angels that are merciful and beautiful. They are led by archangel Raphael, connected to the Sefirah named Hod.

7. **The Elohim:** The angels in this ranking are all about having victory over evil. According to the Kabbalah, they are led by archangel Haniel

8. **The Bene Elohim:** These angels have the sole task of glorifying God. According to the Kabbalah, archangel Michael is in charge of this ranking. More than any other angel, Michael is mentioned in different religious texts, and he is known to be a fighter and a warrior who wants nothing more than to win glory for God. In the Torah, he is known as "the great prince" who fights for those who

love God daily in the battle of good versus evil and the world's end. Michael is connected to the Tiferet.

9. **The Cherubim:** These angels help people when they sin. They want nothing more than to make sure you don't get separated from God because of your sin, and they want you to be as close to God as you can. Gabriel's the one responsible for leading the Cherubim, who played a prominent part in the events after the fall in the Garden of Eden when sin became a thing on earth – thanks to the first man and woman succumbing to the serpent. After the fall of Man, it wasn't enough for God to chase the first couple out of the earthly paradise of Eden. To ensure no one would ever get back in and have access to the Tree of Life, God commanded a Cherubim to be on guard in eastern Eden, and there was also a sword engulfed in flames that zipped back and forth at the entrance. This made any attempt to get back in impossible and a fool's errand. This account is in the Book of Genesis, Chapter 3, verse 24. Remember, Gabriel oversees the Yesod Sefirah.

10. **The Ishim:** There's no other rank of angel as close to humans as the Ishim. They are all about constructing and uplifting the kingdom of God on Earth. They are led by archangel Sandalphon, who is connected to Malkuth.

Other Hierarchies

There are other hierarchies of angels that exist, according to the Zohar, Maselet Atzilut, Berit Menunchah, and Reshit Chochmah.

The Zohar Angelic Hierarchy

There are ten rankings of angels according to the Zohar. These are:

1. Malakim

2. Erelim

3. Seraphim

4. Chayot

5. Ophanim

6. Hashmallim

7. Elim

8. Elohim

9. Bene Elohim

10. Ishim

The Maseket Atzilut Angelic Hierarchy

According to Maseket Atzilut, written by Jacob Nazir, there are also ten rankings of angels, but in a different order than the previously mentioned ones. They are:

1. Seraphim
2. Ophanim
3. Cherubim
4. Shinanim
5. Tarshishim
6. Ishim
7. Hashmallim
8. Malakim
9. Bene Elohim
10. Elohim

The Berit Menuchah Angelic Hierarchy

According to Abraham ben Isaac of Granada, there are ten rankings of angels. He wrote about them in Berit Menuchah. They are:

1. Erelim
2. Ishim
3. Bene Elohim
4. Malakhim
5. Hashmallim
6. Tarshishim
7. Shinnanim
8. Cherubim
9. Ophanim
10. Seraphim

The Reshit Chochmah Angelic Hierarchy

Eliyahi de Vidas wrote Reshit Chochmah, and he also has ten rankings for these beings. Here they are from the highest to the lowest:

1. Chayot Ha Kodesh
2. Ophanim
3. Seraphim
4. Cherubim
5. Erelim
6. Tarshishim
7. Hashmallim
8. Elim
9. Malakim
10. Ishim

Chapter 6: The Teachings of Raziel

The archangel Raziel is the one who is closest to God. Also known as "God's Secret" or The Angel of Mysteries, and being the patron of lawmakers, judges, and lawyers, this archangel holds all the Universe's secrets and understands the mechanics of existence. He is also known as Akrasiel, Ratziel, Galluzur, and Saraquel. The mighty Raziel is a Prince of the Face, and he has several special tasks to perform in the kingdom of heaven. He's never far from God, which means calling on this angel will give you an extra advantage because you can get information that he's picked up in serving God so closely. It's impossible for mere mortals to figure out God's ways because Ein Sof is a mystery that's unknowable, and yet, Raziel may well be the one being who is privy to God's many secrets and actual feelings. Not only that, Raziel makes a point of being helpful to humanity by sharing anything he knows will assist you in life. Specifically, he loves to teach the fact that when it comes to manifesting your desires, all things take root in the world of spirit first before they shoot out into the physical world. Raziel may well be considered the original law of attraction teacher, as he shows one and all that all the thoughts we have are created spiritually and have no choice but to come to fruition in our lives.

Adam and Eve got access to the sacred Sefer Yetzir thanks to the Prince of the Face. They needed the information because life outside the garden of Eden was no picnic, and things had gotten terribly difficult for them. So in his mercy, Raziel decided he would do what he could to help, and he offered the duo his book. However, the other angels were not having it, and they took back the book. Rather than return it to its rightful owner, they decided it was best to let the ocean's murky depths have it forever. After this critical point in the story, you'll learn of other versions of what happened. For instance, some say Enoch found the book, and that was why he lived so long. It's also speculated that he edited the book to include important information about Metatron, a powerful archangel. After this, Raphael became the new owner of the book, then Noah, and finally King Solomon.

Others say that God was sad on behalf of Adam and Eve, and he really wanted to help them. So he commanded Rahab to search the ocean for the book and give it back to the duo. Depending on who you ask, Rahab is seen as an angel or a demon of the deep blue seas. From there, the book was passed on to Enoch, who gave it out as though it were his own work (the Book of Enoch). The next person to own it was Noah, and then it wound up with Solomon, who used it to gain knowledge about magic and manifestation.

The Many Faces of Raziel

Many things can be said of Raziel, but he's well known as the one in charge of the second heaven. Thanks to him, knowledge becomes wisdom. He's shown as a wizard, old and wise, and considered the patron of wisdom. He holds all the knowledge and wisdom and is excellent at teaching those who seek him how to remain focused. He is also good at helping you align with your Higher Self so you can find the connection between you and the wisdom of the Divine. He also shows up as an old man with remarkably huge wings resembling an eagle and a halo that resembles a rainbow. Sometimes he's got a gray, flowing robe, blue wings, and a yellow aura or halo floating around his head. He's the one who understands God's edicts, and he comes to the world so we can learn how to return to the Creator.

The Archangel Raziel is responsible for helping everyone remember important knowledge collected over the ages, including knowledge from previous incarnations. He's the one to call on when you have painful memories that linger and want to move past terrible trauma. If you had made promises in your past lives to people, Raziel could help you break the soul ties so you can be free, and he can also help you become prosperous in life, seeing as he's one of the Angels of Prosperity.

Archangel Raziel in Ancient, Sacred Writings

According to the Kabbalah, Raziel is the patron of Divine Wisdom and the embodiment of it. In other words, he is the Chokmah, the second of the ten holy Sefirot. The Kabbalah holds that Raziel is one of the ten archangels of the Briatic world, the second world of the four created. Rabbinic lore holds that he's the one who penned the Book of Raziel the Angel, or Sefer Raziel HaMalach. In this book, he talks about heaven and earth's deep secrets and mysteries, explaining them in detail. Within the pages of this book is all the knowledge that has ever and will ever exist, in heaven, on earth, and all other realms between. Some speculation exists about the actual author of the book. There are those who claim the author wasn't a divine being, but Eleazer of Worms, while others argue it's Isaac the blind. Many other characters could be responsible for writing the book, including Abraham ben Samuel Abulafia, who had opted for the pseudonym "Raziel and Zechariah. Depending on who you ask, the accounts state that Raziel never gave the first man his book but offered him the Zohar. Those who believe this claim that Hadraniel was the one who God sent to Adam and Eve to let them know the importance of keeping the book and its contents a secret. They were instructed to be careful because it wasn't a good idea to let any of the angels know they had the book with them. Their son Seth became a prophet with great power because Adam let him have the book.

The Legends of the Jews talks about how Noah became so knowledgeable about building arks and how it was thanks to Sefer Raziel, the holy book full of secrets. The archangel Raziel also shows up in Targum Ecclesiastes, explaining the secrets of life to all who will listen each day on Mount Horeb. Look in the Mishneh Torah, and you'll see this angel is there as well, acting as the leader of the Erelim. Some know him as God's own herald, others as the one meant to keep safe the realms unknown and all Ein Sof's mysteries.

It is believed that Noah learned to build his ark from the holy book of secrets.
Currier and Ives, CC0, via Wikimedia Commons
https://commons.wikimedia.org/wiki/File:Noah%27s_Ark_MET_DT4929.jpg

The Sefer Raziel

His book is mentioned once in the Zohar. There, it says that the middle of the Sefer Raziel has a secret writing encoded and that the passage contains 1,500 keys to unlocking the world's mysteries. No one, not even the angels of heaven, knows these keys. This book appears in several other texts, and the fact that it was continually handed down is a clue that there were powerful secrets in it. Other interesting details you can find in the book are the hierarchies of the hosts of heaven and their various purposes, which are essential for all of life to work the way it should. There are also angels that are connected to each sign of the Zodiac. Ovavorial, Lehetial, and Pheniel are connected to Aries, Taurus, and Gemini, respectively. Zorial, Berequiel, and Cheial are the angels affiliated with Cancer, Leo, and Virgo, also respectively. Gabriel's in charge of Scorpio, Medonial rules Sagittarius, and Capricorn is handled by Shenial. Gabriel also rules Aquarius, while Pisces is the domain of Romial. There are at least 70 other angels named in the book. It talks about the lives of the angels, what they are supposed to do, and more. So it's a great source of information on angels. It is believed that Raziel also had another book, the Sefer HaRazim, which he handed to Noah and is known as "the Book of Secrets."

The Book of Raziel the Angel has five sections that deal with the interactions between the angelic author and Adam right after the Fall. Adam had apologized for betraying God, which was why God was moved enough to send Raziel to him. Raziel taught Adam many things, including the proper way to speak and how thoughts have power that has very real effects on both the physical world and your spirit. He teaches about nature's laws, the planets, the way of life on earth, and what life is like in the astral realm. One of the most important teachings the angel had for Adam was how, even though the human soul is enclosed within the physical flesh, it remains a critical path to finding the balance between spiritual and physical realms while living on this planet. Raziel also shared critical information about the Hebrew alphabet and how to work with the 22 letters in magic.

Taking inspiration from various texts, especially the Sefer Yetzirah and the Sefer HaRazim, the Sefer Raziel talks about how all creation and energy start from God-inspired thoughts, which make their way from spirit to physical and manifest through action and speech. The book also shares information about God's names, how to use the stars and the Zodiac in magic, perform protective spells, and work with amulets to heal oneself and others.

Practical Magic

There are various teachings you can learn in Kabbalah as a whole, and when it comes to Kabbalah Ma'asit (Practical Kabbalah), there's much more to absorb. This aspect of Kabbalah is about using magic in practical ways — specifically white magic, not black magic, which is verboten. The tradition of Kabbalah Ma'asit involves chanting the divine names of holy angels, working with amulets, performing divinations, and soothsaying. One of the sacred texts relevant to this tradition is the Sefer Raziel HaMalakh, or the Book of Raziel the Angel.

So, what is this book, really? A single text that's rather long, speaking about all the knowledge there is to be had, from astrology to the secrets of creation on earth. It talks about birth, death, reincarnation, and the life cycle, among other deeply spiritual matters. This book alone is responsible for the difference between mainstream Kabbalah (Kabbalah

Iyunit) and Practical Kabbalah. The former is about trying to understand what God is like and what existence is about. It's about working with a belief system that involves several discourses on God and meditative methods. However, the Practical Kabbalah is about something more. It's about the process of creating using magic and how to reach out or summon the angels and God himself. However, the sacred texts usually condemn working with magic, saying it's evil, so there needed to be a fine distinction between the devil's evil magic and the pure magic of Practical Kabbalah. The practical and theoretical differences are why Practical Kabbalah hasn't been practiced by many other than the Jewish elite.

Using Raziel's Teachings: Working with Thought and Imagination

If there's one powerful thing to take away from the Sefer Raziel, it's that thoughts have power. This is no longer a secret, but despite how often people hear this, they clearly don't put it into practice. Think about how automatic your thoughts are in reaction to things. When something bad happens, notice how quickly you expect more bad things to happen or worse outcomes than what is present. It's very easy to look at things as they seem and assume that's all they will ever be. It's easy to assume that if there's to be any change, it will only be for the worse. However, you've got to master your thoughts. The first step is finding the space between what triggers those less-than-desirable thoughts and your response. You need to stop reacting and start being deliberate about your response, and to do that, you should practice meditation regularly. The more you meditate, the less reactive you will be to occurrences, and the more you'll realize you can choose how you respond — or not to respond at all.

The next thing that one needs to do, in keeping with Raziel's revelation about how thoughts create things, is to practice *thought substitution*. In other words, the next time your mind is tempted to go somewhere, that will only lead to the creation of undesired circumstances, pause and deliberately replace that thought with something you'd prefer to happen. You can either do this each time an errant thought pops up or set time aside each day to see your life or the situation you're dealing with go exactly as you'd prefer. Then, when you see or experience things that point to the contrary throughout your day, return to the memory of your visualization, and learn to accept it as done. By practicing this with all things big and small each day, you'll start to notice the archangel really was correct about the fact that *thoughts create things*. For best results, you should ensure you calm down and relax your body and mind before substituting bad thoughts with preferred ones.

Also, make sure to visualize things that could only happen after you've accomplished what you want, not what happens in the process. For instance, if you want a new car, see yourself driving the car after having it for three months rather than seeing yourself go into the dealership to pick out the car.

Finally, ensure you're playing a part in your mind, just like acting in a movie. Don't imagine yourself from a third person's perspective, or the odds are someone else will get what you envisioned in real life while you're left with nothing. Don't see yourself behind the steering wheel of the car. Instead, see the road ahead, your hands on the wheel, the dashboard in front of you, and so on. *Be in the first person when you think these thoughts.*

Using Raziel's Teachings: Pathworking Ritual for Prosperity and Peace

The ritual is a simple one. Before you start, you must know what you want from the ritual, or it will do nothing for you. Start by writing a request, keeping it a simple statement in the present tense. Assume, for instance, you have been struggling with bad luck in business, and you want to be protected from it. You could write, "Sitael, keep me safe from all that would cause me harm." Don't define how the angel you want to summon should do its job, or the ritual will probably fail because of the constraint you've put on the angel. You must ensure you phrase your intention in the present tense, *not the future* because using the future tense means your goal will always be sometime in the future. You know the saying: Tomorrow never comes. Note that the attitude you have towards this ritual is important. If you assume what you're doing is silly, that means you won't get results.

Here's how the ritual goes:

1. Imagine being in a dark cave.
2. Imagine a waterfall is at the cave's mouth in the distance, and you're now close enough to see the light from the cave's exit.

3. Imagine the sun shining through that magnificent waterfall, forming rainbows. You're still in the dark at this point.

4. Next, imagine you're in a forest full of pine trees and bedazzling light. Feel the light bathing your body, then say, "Raziel." You may notice something immediately or gradually, seeing Raziel or sensing his presence. Either way, don't force it.

5. If nothing happens, you may repeat Raziel's name, not as a mindless mantra but as though you were calling a friend over from the next room. You may do this with your mental voice, which should be clear and loud enough for anyone on the other side of the forest to hear you. You could do this aloud if you prefer. Spend no more than five minutes doing this, and if you haven't received an actual answer, just accept that Raziel is now with you. If you notice her strong presence, stay calm, and don't give a speech about not being worthy.

6. Ask Raziel to lead you to Sitael (or any other angel you'd like to work with). Speak as if you're talking with an old friend you're comfortable with and would be happy to show you where your mutual friend (Sitael, in this case) is.

7. After this, it's time to perform the pathworking for Sitael. Imagine a sword on the ground. It doesn't matter what it looks like. Just see it there.

8. Next, imagine a serpent sliding over the sword.

9. Next, see a field of green grass in your mind's eye, and notice the blue sky.

10. Next, see a tower reach into the sky. This tower is strong and clearly sturdy. It doesn't matter what it looks like, but it has to be obviously built to last, and it must reach into the sky.

11. Call Sitael. Say the name confidently, even if you're not sure you're pronouncing it right. What matters here is your intention. Don't be concerned about doing things wrong regarding rituals like this.

12. If you don't see or feel Sitael's presence, you can call his name several times, either in song or by repeating it. Do this for just five minutes.

13. Whether you had an actual reply or response or not, it's time to make your request. First, think about what you want from the angel. Ensure you feel how much you want it. You want to feel it strong enough that the angel has an idea of how much you want it, but don't feel constrained to drum up deep emotions if you can't manage that.

14. Next, state what you want from Sitael. You may get a response as a flash of an image or feel like the angel needs more information. You just need to trust what you get. You can speak with the angel like a friend. If you want information, it helps to pause after asking to see what you get.

15. After making your request, it's time to end the ritual. Thank Sitael (or whichever angel you just worked with) and Raziel. Then, imagine yourself being back in the dark cave. Don't skip this step.

16. As soon as you're back in the cave, stop imagining and do your best to completely forget and let go of the ritual you just did. Trust that the answer you want will come when you need it, and let it go.

Chapter 7: Kame'ot or Magical Jewish Amulets

The amulet is one of the most vital magic tools in Jewish mysticism and Practical Kabbalah. The Hebrew word for amulet is *kame'a* (plural: kame'ot). In the Sephardic world, many landmark events were marked with folk practices. More often than not, the Jewish scholars and leaders seek to put down folk practices so that they are not tied to superstitious beliefs, but when you pay close attention, you'll notice that the practices in question were part of the fabric of the Sephardic way of life, shed light on the values and concerns of the collective and the individual, and provided useful methods to deal with stressors and anxiety. The Hebrew word *kame'a* suggests that the practice of making and wearing amulets is connected to the concept of binding or tying.

For instance, certain practices became more common during pregnancy. If you were part of the Sepharadim, while you love nothing more than when a new child is born, odds are you're also scared about the danyadores – evil spirits or demons that could threaten the wellbeing of the baby to come. Jewish communities worldwide, whether Sepharadim or Ashkenazim, know that there are things to do to keep the effect of the evil eye away from one's baby and life. A common practice when dealing with pregnant women or childbirth is to spit on a baby (or near them) and then say "poo poo" out loud as an exclamation meant to drive away the evil spirits. The mothers of Salonica had no option but to use special potions and incantations (mastered by the older women among them) to make sure they'd not only carry their babies to term but would deliver them with nothing going awry in the process. There's also a common Turkish practice where, as a pregnant woman, someone would put a sprig of rue by your head to keep you shielded from evil forces and the evil eye.

The Protective Kame'ot

Have you ever wondered how you can ensure you stay safe from such entities as demons? If you thought it was impossible, the fact is, *you can do this*. All you need are the kame'ot. These special, powerful amulets ward off all evil beings from you that may want to wreak havoc in your life. Historically, Jewish women were great at kantikas, but if you wanted a kame'ot, you'd have to go to the men. Some kame'ots would have special parchment put into them, and these are known as *shadayim*. They have the names of the angels written on them, as well as Lilith, who is a demon particularly fond of causing harm to newborns. If you were the mother of the child, you had no choice but to attach a shadayim to yourself and one to your child so that you could both be safe. Since Lilith is a winged being, the Kame'ot accounts for this by incorporating wings, too.

Old World Kame'ot

Back in the Ottoman times, it was common for scribes to craft kame'ot, but just because it was common doesn't mean the practice wasn't powerful. They had various ones that could help summon specific angels meant to protect babies. They would write down these spiritual formulas on special parchment, which is then folded to create a shape reminiscent of the Sephardic filla. Then the kame'a would have to be wherever the newborn is, even when they become adults. Depending on preference, the kame'a could be designed completely sealed off, with a string connected to it to allow you wear it as a pendant. Other times, it's just carried around in a bag or wallet. Some people truly believe that their kame'a is why they can handle all the trouble that comes their way.

New World Kame'ot

Avraham Maimon left his beloved hometown of Tekirag in 1924 because he wanted to be a Rabbi. He decided Seattle was a good place to make his home. He was responsible for keeping most of the Sephardic Studies

Digital Collection of kame'ot, and he kept them in different scripts. What isn't clear is if he's the one who created them. If he did, it would imply he chose to forget about the evil spirits of old when he moved to the United States. Other Sepharadim who had moved to the States still continued to entertain the thought that demons could follow them to their new abodes, so they took their kame'ot seriously.

When it comes to Jewish amulets, they are different from others because there aren't that many symbols on them. The power behind them is the written word. The power also flows from God's names and the angels. For the most part, that's all the amulets draw on for power, but that doesn't mean you can't find other items in Judaism that can act as a magic cure or protection. Sometimes the amulets are fashioned out of stones or parchment. Other times, depending on what you prefer, they could be silver or metal, which means they last longer. Some of them are even cut from gems. There's no hard and fast rule about whether you need to wear it all the time or if you can just hang it up in your home.

Few of the amulets of old are still in production today. When they are, it's only by rare people in specific areas. Other than the Hand of God, most of these amulets are no longer part of popular Jewish practices. Sometimes amulets are really popular, and other times, they aren't. This has been the case over the centuries, depending on where and when. Sometimes, people thought they were nonsense, and other times they believed in them, but they weren't used the way they should be, according to most rabbis.

Approval for Amulets and Amulet Writers

Amulets were a deep cause for concern among religious authorities who didn't like them. Even if not everyone supported them, they have God's names and Torah passages, among other things, making them sort of sacred. They were too sacred to be casually worn or used (like on the Sabbath), yet not so sacred that one couldn't just let them burn in case of a fire outbreak. One thing was clear to the authorities: Amulets were here to stay, and the people weren't about to give them up for anything. So rather than fight the reality of the situation, the authorities simply chose regulation. This meant that before you could write or create amulets, you had to have their approval and verification. How? First, your amulet must have been used for at least three different circumstances by three different people, and it has to be proven as effective. Also, you couldn't just craft your amulet out of whatever materials you wanted. Working with clay, parchment, and metal was considered standard practice. All that mattered was that the parchment was kosher. The content of the amulet also needed to be approved. It wasn't okay to use the Torah's words to heal, but these days, it seems there's more leniency in that regard. It was also fine to protect with the words. As such, most amulets in circulation are more about prevention: Keeping one safe from miscarriage, bad luck, demons, the evil eye, and so on. Some amulets can be used to promote fertility, health, blessings, and favor.

Getting Ready for Amulet Writing

Actual amulet writers who know their craft and have been approved don't just write amulets. Say you write amulets yourself. You've got to get ready because you can't just jump straight into crafting them. There are prayers and rituals you must observe, and if your amulet happens to be made with parchment, you'd be held to stricter standards of preparation. You have to purify yourself, say special prayers, and be on a fast as you script the amulet. You also have to make sure you write any of God's names exactly as it appears in the Torah, and that each letter stands alone without touching the next one. All writing is to be done on the hairless side of the parchment, and before you even get to the writing process, you have to prepare and consecrate the ink for this purpose, too. The scribe also has to recite a blessing to God before writing. The amulet writers are known as *ba'ale shem,* which means "masters of the Holy Name."

Ayin Hara

Ayin Hara means "evil eye," and it's believed to be the source of pain, tragedy, sickness, and all the bad things that could befall one in the world. Often, the harm from the ayin hara results from jealousy, which is why there's a commandment that states one should never covet something that belongs to someone else. A common saying among the Jews is bli ayin hara, which means "without an evil eye." They also say ken eina hara, or keynahora which is Yiddish for "no evil eye," when they are discussing a good thing that just happened. For instance, if you were suddenly blessed with a new and better job than the one you had, you could share that news with your friend and end it by saying, "bli ayin hara."

According to Rashi's commentary, the Torah doesn't talk about the ayin hara, but there are several times the evil eye is at work. This was in the Book of Genesis, Chapter 16, verse 5. Here, Sarah gave Hagar the ayin hara because she was jealous of her ability to carry a child for Abraham, and this was why the maid miscarried. (Notably, she later became pregnant with Ishmael, but scholarly rabbis discovered that Ishmael was not her *first* pregnancy.) Later in Genesis, Chapter 42, verse 5, Jacob warns his sons that they shouldn't be seen together because that could cause a case of the ayin hara against them.

The Talmud and Kabbalah talk about the evil eye. In Pirkei Avot, Rabbi Yochanan ben Zakkai had five disciples offer advice on what they thought it meant to live a good life and stay away from evil. Each Rabbi had a different answer:

- A good eye
- A good friend
- A good neighbor
- To see the outcome of your actions
- A good heart

In response, the Rabbi told them that he preferred the answer given by Rabbi Eliezer, the son of Aroch. What was the answer he preferred? A good eye. He then told them to go and see the worst personality trait that one should stay as far away from as possible. He refers to the evil eye, which leads the heart to evil inclinations and causes one to hate others. There are several ways to stay away from the ayin hara or keep its effects far from you, but most of these are from non-Jewish traditions, dating back to the times of the Talmud when the Jews would have charms to ward off the ayin hara. Some of the ways Jews do this now include:

- Wearing a red thread on the wrist
- Wearing a hamsa or hanging it up at home
- Wearing a chai around the neck

The Red String

The red thread is a sign of vitality and life. The Hebrew word for red is adom, and the word for blood is dam, which is from the same root as the words for "watch," "adam," and "man," making up adamah. The red thread shows the strong connection between life and blood. There's a difference between the color red and the color known as shani. During the time of the Torah, a crimson dye came from a mountain worm known to infest the eastern Mediterranean trees. This insect is called the Torah's crimson worm or tola'at shani. The crimson worm has many connections to the color red and instances where people repented in the Torah, showing that something as insignificant as a slithering worm has an elevated status thanks to the process of repentance. Red is meant to ward off evil, so tying a red string on your wrist will naturally ward off the ayin hara.

The Hamsa Hand

This one sprung from the Middle East, and it looks just like your hand, but with only the three middle fingers pointed out while the other fingers curve outwards. The talisman can be worn as an amulet and offers protection from ayin hara. You may also hang this in your home. Hamsa means "five." It's about the fact that the hand has five fingers, and it's also a representation of the five books of the Torah. Some people call it Miriam's Hand, the hand of Moses' sister. Muslims call it *Fatima's Hand* in honor of Fatima, a daughter of Mohammed the Prophet. It also represents the Five Pillars of Isalm. Scholars think this hand is older than Islam and Judaism, possibly rooted in non-religious origins, but there's no certainty about that. All you need to remember is that kamiyot or Kame'ot represent the concept of binding, the Talmud doesn't outlaw them, and it's okay to have one on you when you're at the synagogue for Shabbat. Sometimes, the thumb and pinky are curved outwards. Other times, they are much shorter than the middle fingers, while they are always symmetrical. Also, there's usually an eye in the middle of the palm that acts as a potent talisman for keeping ayin hara at bay. Other symbols on Hamsa include Hebrew words and the fish, which is also a sign of good luck. Some Hands of Hamsa have mazal or mazel etched into them, and this is meant to represent the concept of good luck.

The Chai

Chai means living, and among the letters in its spelling are Chet and Yud. Some people pair the Chai with the Hamsa Hand, and others wear it with the Star of David. The word Chai is pronounced kai, with the k being guttural. It represents the value of being alive and the hope of seeing another day. It's about having the will to live and the drive to keep all life safe. This amulet can bring you good luck, prosperity, and more.

How to Make an Amulet

1. Get the Hamsa or chai. You can find these for sale online.
2. Cleanse the object by breathing on it thrice.
3. Bless the object with the energy you want to imbue it with.
4. Write the specific blessing or energy you want to carry with you on a piece of paper. You can use any Hebrew letters at this book's end.
5. Wrap the paper around your preferred amulet, then let it stay wrapped for three days and three nights.
6. Wear the amulet.
7. When you sense the energy is waning, you can wrap the amulet in the paper you used to charge it again, leaving it overnight. You can also just do that every night.

Chapter 8: Rites, Rituals, and Shabbat

In Judaism, those who follow the path have to render service to God through having faith, studying his word, praying, being kind to one another, and following the Torah's commandments. Jewish rituals and holidays are all rooted in Halakha, which means "the path one walks." Halakha is Jewish Law. It's a foundation of commandments, rabbinic laws, and traditions. It's not just about religious life but everyday life, including what you wear, how you comport yourself, how you help the less privileged, and so on. The observance of these rites, rituals, and Shabbat is a way to demonstrate your gratitude to and love for God, making each day sacred and beautiful.

Jewish Cycle of Life Rituals

In Judaism, there are life cycle events that are held in high esteem, being honored year after year. Here are some of those events:

Brit milah is also known as *bris*. This is a word etymologically rooted in the Ashkenazic Jews dialect. The Ashkenazi are those who are European but not descendants of Iberia. Bris is the ritual that involves the circumcision of Jewish boys. Circumcision is the process of removing the penis' foreskin days after the birth of a Jewish boy – a practice coming from the story of Abraham's instructions from God to circumcise himself and then Isaac, his son. Once a male child is eight days old, he has to undergo this process (unless there's a medical reason he shouldn't). The bris is carried out by a practitioner known as a mohel. The child must be held by someone (usually the grandfather) who acts as the sandek. Being the sandek is considered a thing of prideAfter this ritual, the family has a meal to celebrate. The meal is called s'udah.

Simchat bat (Hebrew for "joy of a daughter") is a Jewish naming ceremony that is held for a baby girl on the day of her birth or on the first Sabbath after her birth. The ceremony is similar to a Brit Milah (circumcision) ceremony for boys.

During the Simchat Bat ceremony, the baby girl is given her Hebrew name and is welcomed into the Jewish community. The ceremony usually takes place in the synagogue, and family and friends are invited to participate. A Torah scroll is often present, and the baby girl is often held over the scroll as a way of symbolically bringing her under the protection of the Torah.

The ceremony includes prayers, blessings, and the recitation of traditional Hebrew prayers and psalms. The father, or another male relative, may give a short speech, and the baby's mother may also speak. Often, the baby is also blessed by the rabbi, and the parents and grandparents may give gifts to the baby.

Pidyon ha-ben is an interesting event indeed. According to tradition, the firstborn son must help in the Temple in Jerusalem. Since there's no present Temple, the requirement is more symbolic, but the traditional practice is to redeem the firstborn sons from the obligation they have to the Temple where and when possible. The children from families of priests (those born of Aaron, Moses' brother, also called the kohanim, singular kohen) and the Levite families have no choice but to perform their service. Other than that, the father of the firstborn son has to pay five silver coins to a kohen to set his child free once he is a month old. After the ritual, blessings will be recited, and there'll be a special meal.

Bar or bat mitzvahs are for masculine and feminine children, respectively. This is a ceremony that's already covered. It's about the fact that a Jewish child is now an adult. It happens when the boy turns 13 or when the girl turns 12. The ceremony occurs the same day as the birthday, usually during a synagogue service. The celebrant will have to wear a tallit or prayer shawl for the first time in their lives, and they'll have to come up for an aliyah for the first time. They also read from the Pentateuch, and haftarah, part of a book of the prophets connected to the week's Torah portion. They also are meant to give a Dvar Torah, where they talk about what the week's Torah portion means to them. After all this, there's a party or a meal to celebrate.

Confirmation is a ritual that was developed not too long ago, in the 19th century. It's not an obligatory event and is more common with secular Jews. It represents that you've gone on with formal Jewish education, moving past the basic bar or bat mitzvah leve. There are several rituals done to mark this occasion, but usually, the confirmation class is witnessed in the synagogue. Religious gifts can be exchanged, and there's food to enjoy.

Marriage is a complex, intricate ritual when it comes to Judaism. Since there are several ways one could practice Judaism, and since each community treats cultural and religious events differently, you may find all sorts of variations in the practice of marriage. There are many ways that Jews look at non-heterosexual marriages, and these views they hold are still evolving. Trying to get into these views in this book will be too much, so the focus here will be on heterosexual marriages.

In Ashkenazic communities and many others, before the wedding, there's an aufruf. On the Shabbat before the wedding day, the groom is called to the Torah to receive blessings and honor. If the congregation is egalitarian regarding gender, the bride and groom will be called to the Torah. After this, the congregation will sing songs and throw candy at them to signify that they'll have a sweet married life together.

Just before the actual wedding, a ketubah is signed by two witnesses.

The wedding happens beneath a special canopy called a chuppah. This canopy has four poles, and the poles are a representation of the couple's marital home. As the bride, you have no choice but to cover your face with a veil. This is meant to be a reenactment of how Jacob wound up getting married to Leah rather than the one he really wanted: Rachel. To deceive Jacob, there was a veil on Leah's face, and by the time he found out she wasn't Rachel, it was too late. So as a bride, you've got to have a veil, and as a groom, you've got to take the veil off your bride's face to be sure you're getting married to the right partner. The bride has to walk around the groom three or seven times, depending on the community observing the wedding. After this, the groom offers the bride a ring or some other valuable things, and when it's an egalitarian wedding, both partners exchange these valuable gifts. To make the marriage formal, they need the sheva b'rachat, seven blessings. The groom must break a glass, too. If the wedding is egalitarian, both the bride and groom will break the glass, as a reminder that even amid joy, there can be sorry. This practice is a callback to the desecration and ruin of the Temple.

After the wedding, there'll be a party and a festive meal. It's also common for there to be dancing, particularly the hora. Also, there's a traditional practice of lifting the groom and bride in the air on chairs. After the meals, a special grace known as the birkat ha-mazon is recited.

Divorce is yet another event to consider in Judaism. It's not encouraged, but it's allowed. There needs to be a get, which is a document that legitimizes the divorce. According to Jewish law, the husband must offer his wife a get, freely, with no coercion. Tradition also holds that the bride has to choose to accept the get from him, although this is strictly a matter of tradition and not law. This can be an issue in Jewish communities that observe this practice, and as a result, there have been many possible solutions that are sometimes acceptable and other times not, depending on the community in question. These solutions can include prenuptial agreements, but there are fewer legal forms that offer more leeway and creativity every now and then.

Death is an event that cannot be avoided. In Judaism, when someone passes on, they are not embalmed. Instead, the body is washed in a ritual by the chevra kadisha or the "holy society," a bunch of people who will then go on to dress the body in tachrich (a linen garment). Then, the chevra kadisha will put the body into a simple wooden casket. There's to be no metal because the body must return to dust as soon as possible. The group also remains with the body as they recite from the Book of Psalms. When it comes to the funeral, there's no viewing option. It's okay to give eulogies, and you may recite from the Book of Psalms (Chapter 23, in particular.)

Mourning happens immediately after one hears of death. Traditionally, this is when someone recites the following blessing in Hebrew: Blessed are you, Lord our God, king of the Universe, the judge of truth. And then, after this recital, the mourner may rip their clothes. This tradition is sometimes replaced by the mourners wearing a ribbon during the funeral, which they tear symbolically. When the burial is over, it's time for shiva. This period lasts seven days when all are expected to mourn. In English, this is called "sitting shiva." At this time, the family of the one who passed on will receive visitors at their home, share memories of the deceased, pray with the community, and eat traditional comfort foods such as eggs. The mourners aren't about vanity at this time, and any grooming is minimal, at best. Mirrors are to be covered, and no one gets to wear anything fancy — *particularly leather.* They are also not allowed to attend or be part of anything joyous.

After the burial, there's the shloshim, which means "thirty," and lasts for 30 days once the burial is done. The mourners are meant to stay away from anything joyous.

Conversion is what happens when someone non-Jewish would like to convert to Judaism. To do this, you'll need a *beit din* to approve. The beit din is a Jewish rabbinical court. Note that Judaism isn't a movement that goes around trying to add to its numbers. Traditionally, the rabbi is meant to refuse a would-be convert thrice, and they are not to take them under their wing unless the student persists. As a convert, you're known as a ger (for the female, she is called a *giyoret*), and you must study Judaism before your conversion. You must also explain what's driving you to convert to the belt din, who must find your explanation satisfactory. After that, you'll need to immerse yourself in a ritual bath known as a mikveh.

There are various Jewish communities with different outlooks on conversion; some of them don't honor conversions done by rabbis outside their movement. Conversion is something you can do as a gentile if you want to get married to someone Jewish. You can also do this if you were raised Jewish but aren't technically a Jew (maybe because you have a Jewish dad but a non-Jewish mom).

Mikvah or mikveh is a ritual bath, and most Jewish communities have at least one. The law says that you must immerse yourself in this bath to convert to Judaism. Also, if you're a woman getting married, you must go in this bath first. There's also the practice of menstrual purity or niddah, which requires going in the bath. There are many reasons to do a mikvah, and the mikvah is open to men, women, and gender-nonconforming Jews. There's more to the mikvah than already mentioned, as this bath has great symbolism in Jewish tradition. Some Hasidic men practice getting into the mikveh daily, while others do so on Fridays before Shabbat. Some Jewish communities require immersion in the mikvah before Yom Kippur, and others require grooms to go in the bath before getting married.

The mikveh immersions don't need blessings, and they may happen in a mikveh meant for men only, often large enough to contain ten or more men simultaneously. Since they are not necessarily required, most mikva'ot for men tend to be casual, and it could be run without having to schedule a bath as most men are walk-ins. Recently, some progressive Jews have marked special milestones in life with a mikveh, taking baths when there's a special birthday, graduation, bat, or bar mitzvah, and as a sign of starting fresh after loss or pain. For instance, you could take this bath after a year of mourning or dealing with abuse, divorce, rape, or some dangerous sickness you've recovered from. There are usually prayers that follow these baths. There's also the kelim mikveh, specifically meant for immersing dishes so they become kosher. This mikvah is smaller than the other kind and is usually housed in the same building as the larger mikvah.

Holy Days Throughout the Year

The Jewish calendar is lunisolar (keeping in sync with the natural cycles of the sun and moon), and it's used mostly for the Jewish holy days and other traditional observances. The calendar is used to figure out when holy days are meant to be observed. It's also used to indicate the dates for ceremonies like Torah readings, yahrzeits (to honor those who have passed on), Psalm readings, etc. The observances usually commence at sundown, before the date.

Rosh Hashanah is known as the "head of the year." The precise dates depend on when the first day of the seventh month of the Hebrew calendar falls. A special celebration is held during fall, specifically on Tishrei's first and second days. These dates could be anytime in September or October. Note that the Jewish and Western New Years are different on account of the fact that different calendars are used. It's a time for you to think about how your previous year was for you, see how you could have done better, and make a commitment to making the new year better than the previous one. You have ten days to do this, and after that is Yom Kippur. Work is forbidden during this time, and you celebrate the festival with some challah bread and honey, and apples. These sweet treats aren't just randomly chosen, but they are meant to be a sign to you to trust that the coming year will be a sweet one.

Yom Kippur rolls around on day ten of the month of Tishrei. Some call it the Day of Atonement, and just as it sounds, it happens to be the holiest day of the year, and fasting is to be honored with fasting, which is abstinence from food. If you intend to walk the Jewish path, you must realize that nothing matters other than to connect fully with Ein Sof, to find yourself whole in him by being merciful and compassionate to those who have done you wrong while you seek to be forgiven for your misdeeds, too. It's not enough to forgive and be forgiven, though, because you have to confess all sins to God, whose forgiveness is required as well. What's all this forgiveness about? It's about restoring broken relationships between one another and between yourself and God, who loves you. It also matters because, on this day, God comes to a conclusion about what your fate will be. It's a celebration that isn't as upbeat as the others, but it's still a happy and pleasant day because you're seeking to let go of old wrongs and wounds, so everyone can begin on a fresh page with one another.

Sukkot is a celebration that lasts for a full week, and some know it as the Feast of Tabernacles. It's a pilgrimage feast, a period during which the Jews offer their heartfelt thanks to God. Sukkot starts on the 15th of Tishrei. Also called the Feast of Booths, the ceremony is named after the huts or booths known as a sukkah, built solely for that purpose. They represent how the Israelites lived after escaping Egypt with Moses' help, wandering around for 40 years until they came to the promised land. The celebration kicked off as a harvest festival — an ancient one with many traditional practices meant to express gratitude for the bounty of the fall harvest. The sukkahs are made of thatched roofs or branches for the roof. These roofs offer shade from the sun during the day and a gorgeous night sky view. During this time, decorations go on the sukkah. Everyone has myrtle, citron, palm, and willow branches, and they shake them in honor of how God graciously blessed the Jews with the Holy Land and its gifts. If you're part of a Jewish home, it's customary to ask your forbears to share food with you and to stay in the sukkah for as long as possible for the week.

Shmini Atzeret and **Simchat Torah** are ceremonies that last two days. The holy days begin on the eighth day of Sukkot, making up a single holiday for most Jewish practitioners. In Israel, they are celebrated on the same day. The same goes for some Reform congregations, too. The night before both celebrations, the girls and women have to light candles while families say sacred blessings, go to services, and participate in the feasts that happen both night and day. It's unacceptable to do most kinds of work during this time. The event of Shmini Atzeret is when you enjoy your sukkah feast, and some challah is eaten with salt. Before the end of the next day, you enjoy another meal with your family and bid them goodbye after. Hakafot is an important tradition of the Simchat Torah where you and everyone else will march around the reading table in the synagogue while singing songs, both at night before the main event and the morning of the event. Typically, hakafot happens on the eve of Shmini Atzeret.

Chanukah is an eight-day event. Also known as the Festival of Lights, it begins on the 25th day of the month of Kislev, which will often fall in December. The word Hanukkah represents the concept of dedication, specifically celebrating the fact that Judah the Maccabee won a victory over one of Israel's most formidable oppressors, the Seleucids. It's also about the fact that the Temple had been rededicated after this, and it celebrates the story of how the oil lasted seven days longer than it should have in the temple. Chanukah is all about lighting the nine-flamed menorah each night. The entire synagogue and the families who showed up for Hanukkah have to place the menorah in a doorway or window and then pray to God. The middle flame is used to light up the others, with one flame being lit per night until the final night, as all flames burn. After this, the Jews sing songs and enjoy fried meals like sufganiyot and latkes to honor the miracle at the Temple.

Tu B'Shevat is held on the 15th day of Shevat, and it's also known as Rosh Hashanah La'llanot, which means "New Year of the Trees." It usually holds January or February, and it's the end of the rains and the start of the trees' new life cycle in Israel. According to law, this festival is for figuring out the yearly tithes that should be gotten from the food produced. If there are fruits in blossom before this day, the fruits belong to the year before. All fruits that blossom on that day or a day later are New Year fruits. On this day, you're going to celebrate by munching on some delicious olives, figs, dates, and of course, pomegranates. These are the specific foods mentioned in the Torah that you must consume. When you taste these fruits for the first time in the year, you have to give blessings.

Purim falls on the 14th day of the month of Adar, which could fall in February or March. What's significant about this event is that the Jews were rescued from Haman, the terrible Persian prime minister. You'll enjoy not just the retelling of the rescue but plays and kindness from others. On this day, you have the se'udat Purim to look forward to as well. You'll also enjoy the various attires and masks that people adorn themselves with and lovely little cookies as well.

Pesach is the Passover, a celebration of the escape of the Israelites from Egypt. This begins on the 15th day of Nisan, which usually falls in March or April. It's a well-known and loved Jewish holy day. Israelites and Reform Jews celebrate Pesach for seven days, and for conservative and orthodox Jews, the celebrations last for eight days. The eves of the first and second days are kicked off with ritual meals known as Seders. The Seders are accompanied by retelling the Passover story and eating foods that are symbolic. In the Book of Exodus, the Egyptians suffered ten plagues from God because they refused to listen to heed his command to let his people go. Right before God was about to unleash the worst of the plagues he had in store for the Egyptians, where every firstborn son born to an Egyptian family would die, God told the Israelites they had to have a special marking on their doorposts so that they wouldn't lose their own firstborn sons. The marking was to be made with the blood of a lamb. This blood kept them safe as the destroying spirit of the Lord went about reaping the souls of the firstborn Egyptian sons. After the plague, Pharaoh finally gave in and asked Moses and Aaron to get out of Egypt with their people.

Yom HaShoah happens on the 27th day of Nisan. Some call it Holocaust Remembrance Day. This holy day comes a week after the final day of Pesach. Shoah is a Hebrew word that means "utter destruction" and is about the genocide of the Jews in World War II. This day is meant to honor the memories of the millions whose lives were stolen in the Shoah.

Shavuot means "weeks," and it's held over two days. Shavuot is a Jewish holiday celebrated on the religious festival of the same name. It falls on the seventh day of the Hebrew month of Sivan. This unique holiday celebrates God giving Torah to Israel, and there are many customs associated with this celebration in Judaism. It is believed that Shavuot marks humanity's first step towards learning to be master over nature and its blessings. This is celebrated as we retell the events of the Exodus from Egypt and also celebrate God's delivery of the Torah to Israel. The Torah portion read on this day is Bamidbar. During the month of Sivan, you fast for 20 days in preparation for the celebration of Shavuot. The last four days of these are called "Sh'vaot" (or "Shavuot"). The Festival of Shavuot is a three-day celebration, the first day being the most important. On this day, a person must not eat or drink anything that may cause them to become impure. What is prohibited on Shavuot include, but are not limited to: sexual activity, bathing in a mikvah (ritual bath), and eating fruits and vegetables before they have been harvested. The second day of Shavuot is also known as the "Kiddush" day. The Kiddush is a blessing that celebrates the giving of the Torah to the Jewish people. This blessing takes place on this day, and only on this day, before eating anything that may cause the celebrant to become impure, one must say: "May the Lord open my lips, and my mouth shall proclaim Your praise, all day long." One can recite both parts of this blessing in Hebrew or Yiddish. The third day, Sukkot, is a holiday all to itself. This means that those who celebrate Sukkot will not do so on the third day of Shavuot. However, if someone did not celebrate Sukkot during the last month of Tishrei, they are allowed to observe it now. This is declared as such because it celebrates that the Jewish people were freed from oppression in Egypt and were finally able to enter their Promised Land.

Tisha B'Av is the ninth day of the month of Av, and it is a Jewish fast day commemorating the destruction of both Temples in Jerusalem. Its name is derived from Isaiah (59:1) and Jeremiah (2:36), which predicted that the Babylonian and Persian Empires would solemnize this day as a fast. Jews all over the world are encouraged to commemorate, observe, and mourn these tragedies with prayers, fasting, and other rituals. The First Temple was destroyed by the Babylonians under the leadership of Nebuchadnezzar II, in 586 BCE, in what is referred to as the Babylonian Captivity. This was a particularly traumatic time for the Jewish people due to the loss of their nation and temple. Jews who were exiled to Babylon were among those who began observing Tisha B'Av when they returned home after Cyrus permitted them to end their exile. The Second Temple was destroyed in 70 CE by the Romans, led by Titus. This was a much more devastating event for the Jewish people since it resulted in the loss of their homeland and further exile. From then on, Tisha B'Av became a day of mourning for the destruction that visited upon both Temples as well as other tragedies, such as foreign conquest and persecution, which have befallen Jews over the course of history.

Chapter 9: Kashrut and Other Kosher Foods

Jewish mysticism holds that kosher food is food that's healthy for the soul. If you're going to practice Jewish magic easily, you need to keep your soul nourished with the right food because eating is seen as a purification process by the Kabbalah. According to Jewish law, food contains Divine energy, which implies that eating the right meals could help you become more attuned to spiritual matters.

What Is Kashrut?

Kashrut is also known as Jewish dietary law. Kosher foods are those that are in accordance with Jewish dietary laws, which were established to keep kosher animals and to reduce the amount of fat in meat. Kosher is "fit and suitable" or "proper," according to Webster's. Orthodox Jews strictly follow these dietary laws, preparing food for themselves without non-kosher ingredients in the kitchen.

The world over, people are interested in what kosher means, especially why it is so important to the Jewish faith. As with many other religions, Judaism has strict rules concerning food. Although these rules differ from religion to religion, they can be considered some of the basic characteristics of what a kosher diet entails. Using natural and organic ingredients is generally recommended, as is eating less meat and dairy products and more fish, fruits, vegetables, and grains. It also means you can't eat blood from mammals or poultry, nor can you combine meat and milk. There are also things you must not do in the kitchen. Those who want to observe all or some of the rules simply do so to remember their roots.

Many explanations have been given for the different aspects of Kashrut. The Torah tells devotees that to have a good level of holiness, they'll need certain restrictions around food that would set them apart from others. Some explanations are rooted in the different classes of behavior based on Judaism, such as being kind to animals and avoiding animal cruelty. There are also explanations offered by experts that come about from comparing various religions. There's no explanation yet that satisfies everyone, but many of them have helped help Jews observe the restrictions, even when challenging.

Kashrut is rooted in the Torah. It helps you know which animals are fine to eat and that you shouldn't cook a goat's kid In the mil of its mother, among other specific things. The laws keeping you from eating are meant to act as a way to help you be more in alignment with the Torah, and, ultimately, with God. For most modern-day Jews and modern movements, the Kashrut is a matter that can be followed to the extent that the faithful deems appropriate.

Kosher Food

Not every animal or meal is kosher, and you also have to think about whether the animal you're about to eat was healthy and how it was killed. If it wasn't killed humanely, you shouldn't be eating it. You also shouldn't be eating blood, so to avoid that, make sure to soak your meat in salt water. If your fish has scales and fins, it's okay to eat it, but you don't have to worry about any special preparation technique. Not sure about what you're eating? No worries. Several regulatory bodies are in place to check that your food is certified kosher, and when that's the case, there's a symbol on the pack to let you know it's safe.

Eating kosher means combining meat and milk is a no-no, and yes, *that includes pizza.* You have to think about the different ways these combinations can show up in meals so you avoid breaking the rules. Also, you may need to have different plates, pots, pans, and so on for meat and dairy so that there's no cross-contamination. There are some homes where you'll find items that aren't used for either. Kitchenware you don't use for either meat or milk is considered *Pareve,* and if you're using those tools, you can either make meals of meat or dairy. Your kitchen has to be kosher, but don't let that scare you; working within the rules is not as hard as it seems.

Kosher Animals

Does the animal you're about to eat chew the cud? Are its hooves split? Then it's okay to eat it. Among the safe animals are deer, sheep, and cows. The rabbit, horse, and pig are the exceptions to this rule. The slaughter of these animals must comply with *Shechita,* which the Torah describes in detail. It's the fastest way to kill an animal and hurts the least. The slaughter is usually done by a Shochet, who is well-versed in the Shechita laws.

Among the meat that is considered to be Kosher are deer, sheep, and cow's meat.
https://unsplash.com/photos/YlAmh_X_SsE

All fat, meat, and other things from an animal slaughtered in a way that doesn't respect Shechita are not kosher. Any biscuit, cake, or confectionery made with animal fat isn't kosher. All foods that are produced with animal derivatives need to be kosher. After an animal is slaughtered, the Shochet has to check it to ensure no defects. When there is a defect, the animal is *treifa,* which means "torn." The animal is, therefore, not kosher. Usually, the defects are seen in the animal's lungs. Healthy, smooth lungs mean they are Glatt. All non-kosher things are treifa. Regarding birds, the Torah declared that 24 species aren't good for eating, including every bird of prey. You may have turkey, duck, goose, and chicken.

Salted Meat

It's not enough to make sure that a Shochet slaughters the poultry and animals. The Torah explains that getting rid of all the blood from the slaughtered animal is important, which can be done through salting. First, the meat is washed thoroughly and soaked for half an hour in water. After this, the meat is drained on a slanting board and then sprinkled with salt (the medium coarse kind). This way, any residual blood is forced out of the meat. You must ensure the salt is sprinkled on every side. Also, don't skip the cuts and folds in the meat. Let the meat sit on the slanting board for an hour so all the blood can clear out. After this, the meat is rinsed under running water, completely removing the blood. When you're done, the meat is fit to cook and eat. It's obvious why you may not want to buy your meat or poultry from a non-kosher store because even if the animal the meat is from a kosher animal, someone other than a Shochet slaughtered it, which means its meat isn't kosher. Also, the odds are the salting process isn't common outside of Jewish spaces. However, you can buy already packed fowl and meat with a Hensher. This symbol is a kosher one, a stamp signifying the food has had Rabbinical supervision. Rabbinical supervision is when ingredients are checked by a group of Rabbis, who ensure that the ingredients are certified kosher. Usually, this sign will say Kosher Lemehadrin, meaning the product is extremely kosher, which is helpful for those who lean orthodox or conservative in their practice.

Certain parts of the meat in question may have too much blood to be salted enough to get rid of it all, and this is the case with the liver. To eat liver, it should be roasted with an open flame as this is the only way to drain the blood. Some veins and fats, in particular, have to be removed before eating, and the process is known as *Nikkur*. The duties of a kosher butcher, therefore, include:

- Ensuring to only slaughter kosher animals that chew the cud and have split hoofs, as well as kosher poultry
- Slaughtering the animal

- Checking the slaughtered animal for any defects
- Removing the veins and fats
- Roasting liver
- Salting meat.

The butcher and Shochet have to be practicing Jews, and the safest place to buy meat from as a Jew is from a butcher who has a kashrut certificate from a proper Beth Din, which is the Jewish Law Court. Note that shellfish, eels, prawns, and crabs aren't kosher. If there's ever any doubt about what's kosher and what isn't, you should check in with your Rabbi.

Milk

Milk is considered kosher when the source is kosher, too. So it's fine to have goat and cow milk, but you can't have horse or pig milk. These days, there are regulations to ensure that dairy farms are up to code. However, you can be certain that farmers aren't adding non-kosher milk to your regular milk. Still, for most Orthodox Jews, it is important to only have supervised milk — milk inspected by a mashgiach who ensures that bottled milk is strictly kosher. This milk is known as Cholov Yisrael. Cheese must be from a kosher animal, and in the preparation process, you must be sure the rennets are also from a kosher animal. This is hardly the case with commercially made cheese, so it's best to look for cheese with Rabbinical supervision. On the topic of meat and milk, you have to wait six hours after eating meat before you can have anything with milk in it. You should wait three or six hours before eating meat when you've eaten hard cheese. For soft cheese, yogurt, milk, and lighter dairy products, you can wait an hour or half an hour to enjoy your meat.

Veggies and Fruits

Generally, fruits and veggies are kosher. Note that it's not okay to eat fruit if it happens to be part of the yield from the first three years of the tree's existence. Those fruits are known as *Orlah*. If the fruits are from Israel, they must be tithed — this is Hafrashat Terumah Umaaser. During tithe, there's the recital of a special text. Every seven years, Shmittah is held in Israel. Think of it as a Sabbatical year, when there are specific laws regarding veggies and fruits in Israel all through that time. It's not uncommon to find insect-infested veggies and fruits at this time. The Torah is clear about not eating insects, which means you have to inspect your foods for insects — especially those likely to be infested, like dates, lettuce, etc. The inspection is known as Bedikat Tolaim.

Eggs

It's only fine to have eggs that are from kosher poultry. Often, kosher eggs have a pointed end and a round one, but non-kosher eggs are often round all the way. You need to check the eggs to ensure there are no blood clots and throw away the ones with a clot.

Tevilat Kelim

Any item made of glass or metal in the kitchen has to go into a mikvah before you can use it. The same goes for glazed earthenware. Immersing your utensils is called Tevilat kelim, which means "immersion of vessels." Before the immersion, a special blessing is said.

Parev and Wine

Parev literally means neither meat nor milk. Since veggies are considered parev, you can enjoy them with either milk or meat. Everyone has to check if they are milchig (they've consumed milk), fleishig (they've consumed meat), or Parev. For instance, if you had chicken for dinner at 6 PM, you can't enjoy a glass of milk at 8 PM because you're *fleishig* or meaty. When it comes to fish and milk, you're not supposed to cook them together, but you can eat them one after the other right away. You can also have meat and fish together. As for wine, you can only have it under Rabbinical supervision, and the wine should have a Hechsher on it.

Bread

The thing about bread is that most have animal fat or have come in contact with it somehow. Therefore, whatever bread you want to eat, the bakery needs to have been checked to ensure every ingredient is kosher. This is why many Jews will only eat bread made by another Jew. This bread is called *Pas Yisrael.* Jewish bakers who make their own Challah need to set aside a piece of dough in a process called "the separation of Challah" before they bake the bread. Traditionally, that separated piece is offered to a kohen, but now it is simply burned and disposed of properly. There's a special blessing to be said as you separate the Challah, a task that is commanded and often done by women.

Why Kashrut Matters

The Torah has issued explicit instructions on Kashrut, but it gives no clear reason why it's important. Therefore, you can think of Kashrut in one of three ways to motivate you to stick with it. First, all humans are the creation of God. Since God is the grand architect, he should definitely know what would work best for everyone so that all needs can be met, whether those needs are spiritual, mental, or physical. It only makes sense to follow the instructions of the manufacturer of a machine so you can operate the machine efficiently and safely. The same applies when it comes to God and humans. God knows that for the Jews, non-kosher food is terrible. You can, therefore, trust that God's instructions about these meals are for your own good.

Another thing to consider is that you may give your reasons for following Kashrut. For instance, you can realize that you're what you eat, so if you only eat the domesticated, kosher animals, you're likely to take on their good energy and character through the food. Eating wild animals could give you much wilder traits that may not serve you, and also, kosher animals are generally cleaner than the others.

One final point to consider is that you're walking the path of Judaism because you want to return to God, to be so close to him that you might as well be one with him. Therefore, it only makes sense that you should keep his words and abide by his laws so that you, too, can become holy as he is. Also, it makes it very clear that you are God's chosen person. When you doubt what to eat, you can get a Kashrut list from your Rabbi, so there's no doubt in your mind that you're keeping kosher.

Chapter 10: Jewish Meditation and Prayer

As you already know, Hebrew is a divine language. Do you know that each letter of the Hebrew alphabet carries a certain energy you can meditate on? This chapter will teach you all you need to know about working magically with the Hebrew alphabet.

The Power of Hebrew Letters

Jewish tradition holds that the world exists because God spoke it into being. The word of God drives all of creation. Each letter of the sacred language of God acts as a carrier of spirit and life. The Hebrew alphabet is the reason the world continues to turn. These letters have literal meanings as well as deeper, mystical meanings. When you understand each of them, you can glean the hidden mysteries in the Torah and life in general. Studying these letters may cause you to sense a deep connection to spirit that you can't express with ordinary words. Kabbalists are known to meditate on the letters to get a better sense of them and their transformational power. You should take the time to study these letters if you want an even deeper, richer spiritual experience. Know that this chapter is only a starting point and that the practice of studying these letters should ideally be a lifelong matter.

The Hebrew alphabet.
Ieatflower, CC BY-SA 4.0 <https://creativecommons.org/licenses/by-sa/4.0>, via Wikimedia Commons https://commons.wikimedia.org/wiki/File:Magen_David_Hebrew_Alphabet.png

Aleph

This is the first letter of the Hebrew alphabet. It represents number one and the idea of Oneness. It's about achieving Unity with the Divine, and its energy reminds the faithful that everything is one and the same despite the seeming duality of all things. Aleph is a reminder that all things come from the same source and are the same thing, even though they seem separate. It is about the omnipresent, spaceless, timeless existence that can't be divided and that which is perfect beyond understanding.

Beith

The second letter of the Hebrew alphabet, Beith, represents the number and energy of two. As the first letter in the creation story, it represents beginning of duality of Creator/creation – a creation which gives and which receives. Think of Beith as a quantum jump from Unity to duality, allowing for opposites to exist. This letter literally refers to a house, representing the idea of being a vessel or a container. That which is created houses within it the power of the Creator. The physical world serves as a vessel to express God's glory.

In the same way, the physical body acts as the container of the soul. It's the soul that drives the body's being in the world. The dual world still has Unity within it, but the Unity is hidden. Beith is the very root of all buildings, as it contains and then births the letters to come.

Gimel

The third letter represents the idea of harmonizing or balancing out opposites. Gimel acts as a connector between Aleph and Beith, bringing balance to both energies. It's a letter representing the concept of constant change, movement, and transformation, and it literally means "camel." The camel is an animal used to transport people and things, so the Gimel has to do with travel and constant motion. It is the embodiment of both reward and punishment, giving and receiving so that there's always a balance between two things that oppose each other. It also represents the ideas of cultivation, kindness, nurturing, and helping things grow. It's a sign that the Creator is ever generous and benevolent to the created, offering abundant prosperity and life. Gimel represents the idea that blessings flow to those who conduct themselves in a good way while acting unjustly leads to blockages in abundance and goodness.

Dallet

This letter means "door" or "gate," representing the selfless state of being and humility required to go through the doors of your mystery to return to the power of the One or Aleph. Dallet is like a man bent over, representing the idea of being receptive and humble. It's about the structure you need before receiving the good, representing the idea of remaining diligent till you've been blessed.

Sometimes, Dallet is thought of as Dalit, a poor man who has been blessed thanks to the Creator's generosity, as shown by Gimel. It's the awareness that humans have nothing that's truly theirs, as all their wants and needs are fulfilled thanks to the Creator. Even your breath and ability to move are from him and no one else. Dallet is also about structure. Looking at the letter, it looks a bit like a step on a staircase, which you climb figuratively to overcome resistance to study and growth in your practice. If this letter is in your name, it signifies strengths like diligence band the ability to organize, plan, and build.

Hei

The fifth letter of the Hebrew alphabet's fifth letter, it embodies divine revelation. It is God's breath by which he made all of heaven and earth. The word was created as soon as God uttered Hei. This letter represents the idea of life as a gift, and it's that which spells the verb "to be" or Haya, meaning "being." Hei is divinity, the spiritual outcome of life that comes through the previous letters. This letter represents the essence of life within all created things and beings, and it is the idea of effortlessness in how the world continues to turn. It is also about the concepts of specificity, gentleness, and divinity. It's also a representation of the freedom of choice. You can find this letter in the holy name, making it very special among the Aleph-Beith.

Vav

Vav translates to "peg" or "hook," and it is depicted as a simple vertical line, serving a a sort of symbol of the outward projection of God's perfection. This projection is over and within all things created by God, and it makes it possible for him to rule over the affairs of his creation. It's thanks to this projection that the various cycles in life continue unbroken so that mankind can thrive and develop until it's time for God's Oneness and Unity to be revealed to and within everyone. Think of Vav as a sort of hose, allowing a flow of shefa (abundance) from God above to his creations below. It's Jacob's ladder, planted firmly in the ground on earth, with its top in the heavens. It's also seen as Yod's extension, which is where all creation has its origin. The Vav is a lesson on being present, a requirement to connect your physical and spiritual lives. This letter also stands for the number 6, the 6 days of creation, and the 6 physical directions. The physical directions are left and right, up and down, and front and back. The letter is also a phallic symbol meant to bring life, continuity, fertility, and abundance. It is the energy of that which adds.

Zayin

Zayin appears similar to a sword and reminds us of concepts like struggle, sustenance, and spirit. Being the seventh letter, it also represents the idea of Shabbat, the day on which you're meant to rest and tend to your spiritual affairs. From Zayin comes all movement, and it is impregnating energy that causes creation to move. It looks like a Vav but with a crown on it. It is about the struggle between opposites, the fight for existence, and the battle for sustenance.

Heith

This is the letter of infinite possibilities. Think of it like a doorway that turns, allowing you access to higher levels of life in the spirit. It lets you go deep into your soul's mysteries and return to normal waking consciousness. The letter resembles a ladder, showing you that you can break through limitations, which makes sense since it represents the energy of 8, which involves transcending the natural course of things. It's also the embodiment of wisdom.

Teith

Teith means "nest" or "basket" and represents the inherent good in all created. The Teith is a picture of a serpent coiled around a stick. The serpent is the embodiment of the wisdom and knowledge of the serpent in the garden of Eden. The serpent is also a symbol of the healing of the soul, the serpent was lifted up by Moses in the wilderness and whoever looked upon it was healed. The serpent is also a symbol of kundalini energy which rises through the chakras and activates spiritual awareness. The serpent also represents the serpent in the book of revelation that surrounds the throne of God.

Additionally, the letter Teith is associated with the word "tov" (good) and the concept of "goodness" or "virtue."

It is said that the one who meditates on the letter Teith will gain wisdom, understanding, and knowledge. It also represents the power of the spoken word and its ability to bring healing and revelation.

Yod

The tenth letter of the alphabet is a simple point or dot that represents God, from which all things created emerge. It represents Unity even within seeming multiplicity. This is the root of all roots, the Divine Spark that lies hidden within all. This is the spark that causes all things to exist. It's the power of spirit over matter. Yod represents the Creator, whose name starts with this letter.

In the same way, many things happen in the world, but they are all from the one source, that which is indivisible and perfect beyond comprehension. This letter also represents the ten emanations. All things come from Yod and shall return to Yod. It represents that which is beyond space, time, and thought, unperceivable and in one and all.

Khaf

The eleventh letter refers to the cupped palm of a hand stretched out to receive. The shape of the letter is reminiscent of a container, whether a jar or cup. It can be used to receive. As a building houses what happens with the people within it, so does the body act as a house for the energy and life force that animate it. The Khaf is a lesson to shape yourself. Its lessons include humility, letting go of that which causes resistance, bending matter to the will of spirit, and spirit to matter. It's about wise thoughts

---

being put into action to receive concrete results and manifestations. The letter asks you to consider what you constantly contain and change it to attain the preferred reality you want.

Lammed

This letter is a sign of learning and the word for a goad or staff. You can find it in the middle of the Aleph-Beith, so it makes sense that it represents the heart. To learn in Kabbalah, one must do so with heart and soul, for it's not enough to focus only on the mind. The letter shows that spiritual learning is critical to human existence and that everyone is here to learn and express their spiritual lessons through practice in the physical world. When you've dealt with your non-beneficial traits in Khaf, and your ego isn't big enough to interfere any longer, you can learn the perfection of your spirit, master God's laws, and understand his ways so you can live in alignment with him.

Mem

This thirteenth letter represents the Torah and the waters of knowledge and wisdom. It's about manifestation and being willing and able to sink your teeth into the wisdom available to you. It is believed that everyone hungers for God's words, which are life's waters. It's also a representation of the fact that before things can come to fruition, they need time to blossom, and therefore it is important to keep emotions in check and remain humble. This letter matches the energy of the number 40, representing the time required for things to come to fruition. For instance, the embryo needs 40 days to develop fully, the Israelites spent 40 years in the desert before they finally arrived at the holy land they were promised, and Moses needed 40 years to develop and be ready to be Israel's leader.

Nuun

This letter represents faithfulness, the soul, and the idea of something emerging, continuity, fertility, increase, multiplication, and humility because it bends at the top and bottom. Some consider it a symbol for the 50 Gates of Wisdom of Binah. Nuun is about remaining present and how the soul stays humble, silently offering its light but remaining in the shadows. Nuun is an illustration that to follow the Creator's will rather than your own ego, you need to bend above and below. This letter also demonstrates the relationship between the impermanent body and the permanent soul. In Aramaic, it means "fish." So, the letter is a lesson on how to flow and remain flexible like fish when it comes to change.

Samekh

Samekh represents memory, protection, and support. The circumference of the letter shows God, while the inner part is God's creation, whom he keeps safe and supporting in all they do. The letter represents the Ohr Makif, the Surrounding Light of Kabbalah, a representation of God's providence that continues to encompass and drive all of existence. Samekh is that which contains the form of all things. It's a lesson on circular thinking, asking you not to think only for yourself but for the good of everyone. This is the process of thinking with your soul and being inclusive, as you learn each day that wisdom doesn't just lie in one container but is in everyone. The Samekh is a lesson that to know God, you must let go of the self-imposed limitations on your mind. You've got to drop everything you think you know about how life works and dare to disregard the physical world and its limitations so that you can know who you really are. When you can cleanse yourself of negativity and limited thinking, master your ego, stay humble, and keep your ears open to the voice of your soul, it's worth it. You will find you're always supported, protected, and helped at every turn. Nun combined with Samekh is Nes, and this means "miracle." Knowing the lessons Nuun and Samekh have for you, you can discover and make miracles happen.

Ayin

This letter means "eye, "so it involves vision and revealing previously hidden lights. Ayin asks you to look beyond, and it is also about time. It's about being a visionary. You've got to keep your focus on the present as well as the future. The proper pronunciation of the word Ayin gives a guttural sound that activates the thyroid gland. Ayin is a part of many words that have to do with the concept of time. Some of these words are:

- Eternity
- Till
- Moment
- Past
- Future
- Hours
- Time

Ayin is a lesson that teaches that you need to understand cause and effect and how your present choices and decisions can affect the results you get in the future. It asks you to keep your eyes open and see beyond what is physical as its energy takes you from the darkness into light. It's about seeing through the darkness of limitations to the good that isn't visible yet.

Peh

Peh is a letter that means "mouth." The Kabbalah considers speed to be a spiritual ability that can be used to give life or cause death. You are what you think, and what you think is what you speak, meaning your words can give you a new reality. The quality of your speech is a mirror of the quality of life you live. Peh is a lesson on choosing your words wisely and not wasting them creating situations you don't really want.

There's a quote from the Talmud Baba Messiah that says, "Don't say one thing with the mouth and another with the heart." This is the lesson Peh teaches all. Use your words to speak your destiny into being. Awaken your spirit with the right thoughts and proper speech.

Tsadde

Like other Hebrew letters, the Tsadde is also associated with certain meanings and interpretations. The Tsadde is formed by two Hebrew letters, 'zayin' and 'dalet' which resemble a fishhook, this shape can be connected with the word "tsadik" (righteous) or the concept of "righteousness." A fishhook is also a symbol of something that catches and holds on, in this way it represents the ability to hold on to righteousness and maintain it.

Additionally, the letter Tsadde is associated with the word "tzaddik" (a righteous person) and the concept of "righteousness" or "justice." It is said that the one who meditates on the letter Tsadde will gain righteousness, justice and the ability to hold on to righteousness.

It is also the letter of the Zohar, the book of splendor, which teaches the secrets of the creation of the universe and the human soul. It is said that the one who studies the Zohar will gain wisdom and understanding of the spiritual dimension.

Khof

This letter is called Qof or Kuf. It may refer to a needle's eye, as well as the back of one's head. Khof is also a word for "monkey," representing the sacred and profane (Kedushah and Klipah). The husk or peel represents all the negativity in this created world. Khof is about needing to take this peel or hist away to show what is holy and lies within you. As Khof means "monkey," it also represents the human who hasn't mastered their base instincts and is still animalistic, with no higher thinking faculties. This letter is a call to rise above the animalistic tendencies in humans so that they can be more like God. Khof is the one letter in the Aleph-Beith that stretches below the other letter's line, which represents the idea of going into the lower world and the chance to ride from there. Kuf also means circle, which is about nature's many cycles. It's a reminder that your life has cycles, and you must change and evolve to uncover your full spiritual light.

Reish

It is said that the Reish represents the head, as it is the first letter of the word "rosh" (head). This meaning can be connected to the idea of leadership and authority.

Additionally, the letter Reish is associated with the word "rachamim" (mercy) and the concept of "mercy" or "compassion." It is said that the one who meditates on the letter Reish will gain compassion and mercy, and will be able to extend compassion to others.

The word "Reish" also has several meanings in Hebrew, depending on the context. Some of the most common meanings include "head," "leader," "boss," "chief," "prince," "ruler," and "first." In some biblical texts, "reish" also refers to the beginning or the top of something.

It is also the letter of the God's name El-Roi, the God who sees, and the letter of the word Rabbi, which means teacher or master.

You can break through challenges, break things down into their smallest units, and build something new from scraps. Reish is also connected to the Reshimo, representing the spiritual DNA everyone is meant to express and discover in life. Within Reish are the secrets of the beginning or Beresheet. The letter also represents the secrets contained in Keter, the highest of all Sephirot.

Shin

Shin is about transformation and fire. The Shin is formed by three Hebrew letters, which resemble the shape of a tooth and it is the first letter of the word "shinayim" (two) and "shalom" (peace)

Additionally, the letter Shin is associated with the word "shaddai" (Almighty) and the concept of "Almighty" or "all-powerful." It is said that the one who meditates on the letter Shin will gain the power of the divine, and the ability to manifest their desires.

It is also the letter of the word "shamayim" (heavens) and the letter of the name of God as "Shaddai" (Almighty) and also the letter of the word "Shekinah" (The presence of God).

The Shin has a special significance in Kabbalah, where it is believed to represent the three sefirot of wisdom, understanding, and knowledge. It is also associated with the element of fire, which is often associated with God's presence, and is often used to represent the divine spark within each individual.

Tav

The last letter of the Aleph-Beith, this one means "seal," "omen," "sign," or "mark." It represents the idea of completion. It's also about perfection, truth, and the Tikkun's respiration. It's a call to come back to your life's purpose, complete it, and start over with Aleph's Oneness. The Tav is a revelation that even from the beginning, there was an end waiting to be experienced. It's the last letters of the Beresheet, too. This letter teaches that all things were put in place by God to get one and all to a final level of being perfect. This is where all creation can be truly fulfilled. It's the completion of the real truth. As soon as Tav has been accomplished, one has no choice but to go back to Aleph, as all life is a cycle. Aleph is the source of all things and the beginning. Tav is never actually the end but the start of new things.

How to Meditate on Hebrew Letters

Contemplating these letters offers you a connection to God and his power, which you can use to change your life for the better. Here's a simple exercise to meditate on any letter you want:

1. First, look at the letter. Do this for five minutes, studying its form. You're practicing "engraving" or chakikah, which will help you see the letter so clearly that it doesn't move or waver when you envision it.

2. Shut your eyes and bring the image of the letter to your mind's eye. Initially, it might be a bit of a struggle, but don't let that stop you.

With time, you'll be able to hold the image in your mind for longer.

3. If you notice other images in your mind's eye, that's fine. Just focus on the letter until that's all on your mind. This process of removing the other images by focusing on the letter is called chatzivah or hewing.

4. Let the image sit in your mind for fifteen minutes. If you need to remind yourself of what you're supposed to be seeing, you can open your eyes to take in the image and then go back to see it in your mind's eye. If you're still struggling with other images in your mind, see the letter a being black against a white background and cut out other things around it. Take your time with this. With each practice, you'll get better.

It is important to note that you shouldn't concern yourself with the results of this meditation. Do this daily for thirty days, and you'll be amazed at the results.

Prayers for Sephiroth

Note that you can make these prayers as long or as short as you want, and you can simply repeat a phrase over and over if you prefer, contemplating the meaning of what you're saying.

Keter: Ask God to connect you with the spiritual realms and thank him for doing so.

Chochmah: Ask God to grant you the wisdom you need to achieve your vision.

Binah: Ask God to give you deep understanding. You can contemplate the Binah when you're dealing with a matter that has you confused or when you want more light about what a certain portion of the Torah means to you.

Chesed: Ask the Creator to show you how to be benevolent and kind as he is.

Gevurah: Seek the Divine's help with his power so you can change things in your life. Alternatively, you can pray for the ability to exercise restraint.

Tiferet: You can ask God to show you the beauty and harmony in the worst of situations, or in yourself, or in someone else.

Netzach: Ask God to manifest himself triumphantly in whatever situation you find yourself in. You can also pray for endurance to go through life.

Hod: You can pray for God's glory to be evident in your life or ask that you have a life where you can hold your head high in dignity.

Yesod: While focusing on this sefirah, ask God to help you live a righteous life so you have a solid foundation to build your relationship with him.

Malchut: You can pray to God to make his presence unmistakable in your life so that your life is one full of miracles, mercy, kindness, love, blessings, and abundance.

Extra: Jewish Terms You Should Know

Many terms in Hebrew underscore important aspects of Jewish mysticism. You should know what they are so that you can work with them with understanding.

Hebrew – The language spoken by Jews. The Hebrew language was originally written in square Hebrew characters, but through the years has later developed into a more common alphabet. Throughout its long history, changes have been made to the alphabet and its various forms of punctuation and script.

Qabalah - This is the name given to a form of Jewish mysticism that is based on the concept of creation. Qabalah goes into detail regarding the nature of God and what it is that He created, which in turn, helps us understand ourselves.

Torah - This is the word used in the Jewish language to refer to the first five books of the Bible. The Torah begins with Genesis and ends with Deuteronomy. Originally, it was not called the "Talmud" until it was later combined with the Talmud into a single book.

Tanakh - This is the name given to the Jewish Bible. Tanakh means "The Law or Teaching" in Hebrew. It consists of three main divisions: Torah, Nevi'im, and Ketuvim. These three main divisions are further subdivided into the various books that make up these divisions.

Mishnah - This is a collection of Judaism's Oral Laws, which were created around 200 CE by Rabbi Judah HaNasi and his colleagues after they codified the oral tradition of the Torah. These laws were based on scripture but also included some statements concerning how Israel should live during their period.

Tzitzit - Is another Hebrew word for "fringes."

Halakha - Is the Jewish Law. Jewish laws help define many things in Judaism, such as a proper Sabbath meal and how it should be prepared.

Challah – Is a type of bread that is made without yeast. Its name comes from the Old French word "Lacaille," which came from the Latin "Laicola" and means "loaf." This bread contains eggs, sugar, oil or butter, and water.

Chumash - This is another Hebrew word for "five," which in the Jewish faith is used to describe the five books of the Torah.

Halachot - This is another Hebrew word used to describe Jewish laws.

Kosher – This means "fit" or "proper." Today, kosher is often associated with dietary laws that are set by Judaism and followed by religious Jews. To be considered Kosher, food must be prepared according to specific rules and regulations. Kosher comes from the Hebrew term for fit and proper, "kasher."

Shabbat – Is another Hebrew word for Sabbath. Shabbat is a part of the Jewish faith and observance of God's laws. It is a day that all Jews are encouraged to keep as close to their religious beliefs as possible.

Rosh Hashanah – Is the Festival of Trumpets or New Year. The name refers directly to the sound that is heard on this day. Expect the Festival of Trumpets at the end of September.

Yom Kippur – Is the Day of Repentance. This holiday occurs in mid-September and is a very solemn, holy time for Jews, where they fast and pray for their sins committed throughout their yearlong lives.

Chassidic – This is a term used to describe a group of orthodox Jewish sects and traditions. The first use of the word "Chassidism" can be traced back to the Eastern European Jews in the 18th century. These Chassidic groups were typically known for their long beards and dark clothing.

Yeshiva – This is another Hebrew word that is used to describe an academy or college dedicated to studying Torah and other religious writings, such as Chassidic literature. Yeshivas are typically located in

Israel, attracting men who want to become rabbis and Jewish teachers.

Rabbi – This is another Hebrew word for Rabbi. It is often used in comparison with "Reb" or "Rabbi" to describe someone more learned or better qualified than the other person. Today it is a widely used term, particularly by Jews and non-Jews.

Pesach – Is another Hebrew word that means Passover or Passover Festival. It refers to the celebration of the liberation of the Israelites from slavery in Egypt. This festival gives Jews a chance to reflect on their freedom and thank God for it by eating matzo, a holy food.

Chavurah – Is another Hebrew word that has been used to describe a group of Jews who are collectively bonded by their faith. Today, the word is less commonly used than in previous generations and is typically reserved for the most closely knit of Jewish communities.

Shalom – In Hebrew, Shalom means peace, but it can also be used positively to describe people who are kind and want to help others. The word is sometimes misused today to refer to non-Jews or non-Jewish activities.

Mitzvah - This is an alternative spelling of the word Mitzvot, another Hebrew word for commandment. In Judaism, this refers to a specific religious rule that Jews must follow.

Matzo – Is an unleavened bread that is eaten on Passover. It is made with flour and water and baked in a very hot oven that kills all of the yeast, which would make it rise. Matzo can also be used as a way to replace leavening during other Jewish holidays or funerals as well.

Bar Mitzvah - It is the term that is typically used to describe a Jewish boy who is becoming a man. This ceremony is on his 13th birthday as a symbol of his entrance into adulthood in the eyes of God.

Bat Mitzvah - It is the term that is typically used to describe a Jewish girl who is becoming a woman. This ceremony is on her 12th birthday, and it marks the entrance of young womanhood into the life of God.

Kiddush - This prayer is for all Jews. They recite to praise God and show their thankfulness for His many blessings. The prayer is recited before every meal.

Kashrut - This is another Hebrew word that refers to the laws and rules of keeping kosher food, which is set forth by Judaism and followed by religious Jews and other people who follow Jewish traditions.

Teshuvah - Is a Hebrew word that refers to repentance and is used in the Jewish faith to describe spiritual reforms and conversions.

Beit Din - Is another Hebrew word for religious court. In Judaism, Beit Dins are courts established to judge disputes between Jews living in Judea during the era of Jesus' birth and death or with other Jews or non-Jews when there are criminal or civil issues involved.

B'nai Mitzvah – This is a Hebrew word that refers to a Jewish person who is learning about Jewish law, though it can also be used to describe a Jewish girl who is becoming a woman. This ceremony marks the entrance of young womanhood into the life of God by celebrating her transition from childhood to womanhood.

Tallit - This Hebrew word refers to a prayer shawl worn by Orthodox Jews. It is also referred to as a tallit katan or a "prayer scarf." This cloth was traditionally made out of wool, but it can be made from other materials today.

Tefillin - This is another term for tefillin, which are small black boxes that have been used for centuries to hold Jewish scriptures. They contain verses from the Torah and are customarily worn by both men and women on their arms and heads during morning prayers.

Kippah - This is another Hebrew word that describes a Jewish skullcap worn by all Orthodox Jews.

List of Hebrew Letters

1. Aleph
2. Beith
3. Gimel
4. Dallet
5. Hei
6. Vav
7. Zayin
8. Heith
9. Teith
10. Yod
11. Khaf
12. Lammed

13. Mem
14. Nuun
15. Samekh
16. Ayin
17. Peh
18. Tsadde
19. Khof
20. Reish
21. Shin
22. Tav

Part 2: Kabbalah

Unlocking Hermetic Qabalah to Understand Jewish Mysticism and Kabbalistic Rituals, Ideas, and History

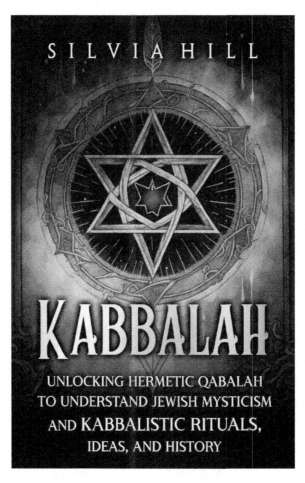

Introduction

Have you ever wondered what the Tree of Life is? Or what is Kabbalah all about? If so, this book is for you!

Kabbalah – a way of thinking and being spiritual that has grown from Judaism – teaches about the divine nature of the universe, how people relate to God, and how to grow and find spiritual fulfillment. Despite its ancient origins, Kabbalah is not just for Jews – it is a system of thought and universal knowledge that can be studied and practiced by people of any religion or background.

The term "Kabbalah" is derived from the Hebrew root word "to receive," which refers to the act of receiving divine knowledge. Kabbalah is often called a "mystical" tradition and has some mysteries and secrets. But at its core, Kabbalah is a practical system that can improve your life and relationships and help you find meaning and purpose in the world.

The concepts and symbolism of Kabbalah can be found echoed in many different cultures and religions, including Christianity, Islam, and Buddhism. It has recently become increasingly popular in the West, especially as well-known celebrities have voiced their interest in the system. While Kabbalah has been gaining popularity, there is still a lot of misunderstanding about what it is.

Most people think of Kabbalah as a form of magic or witchcraft, *but this is incorrect.* It's not about performing spells or rituals; it is a system of thought that can be used to understand and interpret the world around us. Kabbalah is often linked to the Jewish mystical tradition, but it is not just for Jews; Kabbalah is a *universal system that people of any background or religion can study and practice.*

This book begins with an introduction to the basics of Kabbalah, including its history and practical applications. We'll discuss who can become a Kabbalist, the Tree of Life, and what it has to do with the belief system. Then, we'll explore some of the critical concepts of Kabbalah, such as the Sephirot and the 22 paths. You'll also learn about the different worlds of Kabbalah and how to apply Kabbalistic principles to your everyday life.

By the end of this book, you will better understand what Kabbalah is (and isn't) and how you can use its teachings to improve your life. You will also learn how to bring Kabbalistic ideas into your everyday life through rituals and practices to make you feel more peaceful, clear-thinking, and aware of yourself. Whether you are new to Kabbalah or want to learn more about this ancient system of thought, this book is the perfect introduction.

Chapter 1: A Brief History of Kabbalah

Kabbalah is a Hebrew term that means "to receive" or "receiver." This refers to the act of receiving knowledge or wisdom from a source outside of the individual. There are many different spellings of the word Kabbalah, such as Qabalah or Cabbalah. However, the most commonly used one is Kabbalah. No matter the tradition, this spelling will be used throughout the book to keep things clear.

The Star of David.
https://commons.wikimedia.org/wiki/File:V08p252001_Mizrach.jpg

This chapter will discuss where Kabbalah came from and how Jewish mysticism, Hermeticism, and the Order of the Golden Dawn interpreted it. It's crucial to note that there is *no single correct interpretation* of Kabbalah. Instead, each tradition has its unique way of understanding and using knowledge. Readers are encouraged to study each tradition and find the one that resonates with them the most.

What Is Kabbalah?

Mystics "...want to taste the whole wheat of spirit before it is ground by the millstones of reason." ~ Abraham Joshua

Kabbalah is a system of Jewish mysticism and magic that includes ideas and practices from many different sources, including the Bible, the Talmud, and ancient pagan traditions. Again, the word *Kabbalah* comes from the Hebrew word for "receiving," which refers to the idea that wisdom can be received from God or other spiritual beings. Kabbalistic beliefs and practices vary widely, but they involve studying biblical texts, meditating on mystical diagrams called "sefirot," and performing magical rituals.

Many Kabbalists also believe in reincarnation and the transmigration of souls. Kabbalah has affected many parts of Judaism, including how the Torah is read out loud in synagogues. Celebrities like Madonna and Britney Spears have also popularized it. While some Kabbalists believe their teachings should be kept secret, others have published books and created websites to share their beliefs with the world.

The Origins of Kabbalah

Kabbalah is a Jewish mysticism system that started taking shape in the 1200s. While it shares some commonalities with other mystical traditions, such as the belief in the existence of an unseen reality, Kabbalah also has a unique history and set of beliefs. One of the key figures in the development of Kabbalah was Isaac Luria, who taught that the universe had been created through a process of *tzimtzum*, or divine self-withdrawal. In Lurianic Kabbalah, God is seen as being inside and outside everything. Here on earth, people have the potential to work with God to make the world a better place. Kabbalah is still practiced by many Jews today as a way to get closer to God and figure out what Jewish traditions are really about.

Early Origins

Kabbalah is thought to have started in ancient Babylonia, where Jewish mystics created a system of theosophy or divine wisdom. This system was later elaborated on by the rabbis of the Talmudic period. Kabbalah first began to develop as a distinct field of study in the 12th century in the Spanish city of Toledo. Ibn Gabirol's neo-Platonic philosophy and Ibn Arabi's Arabic mysticism influenced Jewish philosophers and mystics at this time. These thinkers attempted to synthesize Jewish tradition with the ideas of Plato and Aristotle.

The Zohar

The Zohar is the central text of the Kabbalah, a mystical tradition within Judaism. It is a book of allegorical stories and teachings meant to be interpreted on multiple levels. On a literal level, the Zohar tells the story of how the world was created and the fall of Adam and Eve. On a more spiritual level, it teaches about the nature of God, the relationship between man and God, and the path to salvation. The Zohar also provides insight into Jewish law and tradition. It is a very important piece of literature and a religious and spiritual teaching text. Its vivid stories and powerful images have been a source of ideas for artists and writers for hundreds of years. Kabbalists still study the Zohar today for what it says about religion and how well it is written.

Kabbalah in the Middle Ages

The Middle Ages were a time of great religious upheaval. With the rise of Christianity came the rise of new religious movements, including Kabbalah. Kabbalah teaches that God can be understood through mysterious symbols and hidden meanings. During the Middle Ages, the movement grew in popularity, especially among people who spoke Hebrew in Spain and Portugal. Even though the mainstream rabbinical establishment was skeptical of Kabbalah at first, it eventually won over many followers. Kabbalah greatly impacted Judaism, and its teachings still significantly impact both Judaism and Christianity today.

The 16th Century and Beyond

The Kabbalah says that the Torah has a hidden meaning; if people can figure out what it is, they can get closer to God. Kabbalists believe the Torah is like a tree, with each letter corresponding to a different branch or leaf. Kabbalists use many different methods, like gematria (*computing the numerical value of words*) and notarikon (*a cabalistic way of deriving a sentence from a single word*), to figure out the hidden meanings of the Torah. Once, only small groups of educated Jews were interested in Kabbalah. But recently, it has become more popular; celebrities and non-Jews are turning to its teachings for spiritual guidance.

In the 1600s, the Sabbatian crisis shook up the Jewish community. During this time, many Jews followed the false messiah, Sabbatai Zevi. He claimed to be the Jewish Messiah everyone had been waiting for, and his followers thought he would save them. But Zevi became a Muslim, which, understandably, made many of his followers lose faith in Kabbalah. In the 18th century, the Sabbatian crisis led to the start of the Hasidic movement. Hasidism sought to revive the spirituality of Kabbalah, and its followers believed that Kabbalah could help them achieve a close personal relationship with God. Hasidism is still an important part of Judaism, and its teachings have helped shape how people think about Kabbalah today.

Kabbalah in the Modern World

Kabbalah has experienced a renaissance in the modern world. Thanks to the work of thinkers like Rabbi Isaac Luria and Rabbi Moshe Cordovero, Kabbalah has been reintroduced to the mainstream Jewish community. Likewise, it is becoming more well-known among non-Jews who are simply interested in its mystical teachings and are drawn to Kabbalah's emphasis on personal spiritual growth. Its teachings have been featured in popular books like The Secret and The Da Vinci Code. As interest in Kabbalah continues to grow, its impact on the world will likely become even more pronounced.

Kabbalah in Jewish Mysticism

Kabbalah is a central component of Jewish mysticism. It is a tradition that says people can get close to God and talk with Him directly. *(Note: for consistency, we will use "Him" and "He" throughout this book, understanding that many believe God to be female or genderless.)* Kabbalah is based on the belief that there is a hidden meaning behind the Torah and that by understanding this hidden meaning, humans can achieve a personal connection with God. Kabbalists believe that the Torah is like a tree, with each letter corresponding to a different branch or leaf. As mentioned before, Kabbalists use many different methods to discover hidden meanings within the pages of the Torah.

Jewish mysticism has its roots in the ancient world. The first time Jewish mysticism is talked about in writing is in the book of Exodus when God gives Moses the Ten Commandments. Jewish mystics have tried to get to know God through prayer, meditation, and study for hundreds of years. In the Middle Ages, Kabbalah emerged as a major force in this quest for knowledge.

Kabbalah in Hermeticism

Hermeticism is a separate religious and philosophical tradition that also says people can have a personal relationship with God. Like Kabbalah, Hermeticism is based on the idea that the universe has a hidden meaning and that if people can figure out what it is, they can unlock its secrets. Based on principles from Hermes Trismegistus, it uses various methods to understand the hidden meaning of the universe. These methods include astrology, tarot, and numerology.

Hermeticism has its roots in the ancient world. The first recorded instance of hermeticism is found in the Emerald Tablet, a text purportedly written by the Egyptian god Hermes Trismegistus. Throughout the centuries, Hermetics have sought to experience the divine through magic, alchemy, and other esoteric practices. During the Renaissance, thinkers like Giordano Bruno and Cornelius Agrippa spread the ideas of Hermeticism, which became a major force in Western thought. In the modern world, hermeticism has experienced a resurgence in popularity, with people turning to its mystical teachings in search of guidance and spiritual enlightenment.

Kabbalah in The Order of the Golden Dawn

The Order of the Golden Dawn is a secret group that teaches its members how to do magic and get in touch with the divine in a personal way. Like the other belief systems, The Order is based on the belief that the universe has a hidden meaning and that humans can achieve a personal connection with the divine by understanding this hidden meaning. The Order of the Golden Dawn teaches its members how to use astrology, tarot, and numerology, among other things, to figure out what the universe is really all about.

The Order of the Golden Dawn has its roots in the Victorian era. In 1887, a group of British occultists who were interested in Hermeticism's magical teachings started the Order. It quickly became Britain's most influential secret society, with members like William Butler Yeats and Aleister Crowley carrying its teachings to the wider world. The Order of the Golden Dawn lost popularity in the 20th century, but its teachings have continued to influence occultists and mystics worldwide.

How Can We Learn from Any Tradition?

There's always something to learn from other cultures, whether it's their art, music, philosophical traditions, or simply the way they live their lives. One of the best ways to learn about another culture is to travel there and experience it first-hand. This can be difficult or impossible for some people, so another way to learn is to read about other cultures, watch documentaries, or even visit cultural centers or museums. Whichever method you choose, make sure you approach learning about other cultures with an open mind and a willingness to see things from a different perspective. Only then can you truly begin to understand and appreciate the beauty of diversity.

1. Do Not Take What Is Written as Truth

Many people think that they can only learn from their own traditions. However, this is not always the case. It's possible to learn from any tradition as long as we approach it with an open mind, curiosity, and a willingness to question what we read. When we take something at face value, we are more likely to blindly accept it as truth. However, when we critically engage with a tradition, we can learn a great deal by looking at its history, culture, and beliefs. In addition, by looking at a tradition through a critical lens, we can gain a deeper understanding of our own beliefs and traditions. So, the next time you hear about a new tradition, don't be afraid to ask questions and look at it closely. You may be surprised at what you learn.

2. Consider the Source

Countless traditions around the world have been passed down through generations. These traditions give us a window into the past and a connection to our heritage, from religious ceremonies to cultural customs. But as times change, some traditions may no longer be relevant or appropriate. So how can we learn from tradition without being bound by it?

One way to approach this is to consider the source of the tradition. Where did it come from, and why was it created? For example, many traditional gender roles were based on the idea that women were weaker and less capable than men. But now that we know better, we can question these outdated assumptions and create new traditions that are more equal and inclusive.

Another important thing to consider is whether the tradition is harmful in any way. Some traditions may seem harmless at first, but they may be sexist, racist, or homophobic when you look at them more closely. If a tradition is causing harm, an open discussion needs to be held about finding a remedy and how to implement it.

Finally, we should also be respectful of other cultures and their traditions. We can still learn from their customs and rituals even if we don't agree with everything they do. By doing so, we can create traditions that are more meaningful and relevant to our lives.

3. Study, Experiment, and Discern for Yourself

One of the great things about traditions is that they connect us to the past. They can offer us a sense of stability and belonging in a world that sometimes feels uncertain. However, traditions are not static; they evolve to meet the needs of those who practice them. If we want to learn from tradition, we need to be willing to study it. We can experiment with it and ultimately discern for ourselves what is helpful and what is not. By doing this, we can ensure that our traditions are still important and alive and learn more about the world around us.

4. Go within for Understanding

There are many ways to learn about and understand the world around us. One way is to look to the past and learn from the traditions of those who came before us. Another way is to go *within ourselves* for understanding. Each approach has its benefits and drawbacks, but both can be useful in different situations.

Looking to the past can give us a better understanding of where we come from and how we got to where we are today. It can help us see the interconnectedness of all things and how our actions have ripple effects extending far into the future. However, it can also be easy to get caught up in nostalgia or dwell on how things used to be "better." To truly learn from tradition, we must be willing to question why things are done the way they are and whether there might be a better way.

Going within ourselves for understanding can help us find our truth and develop our unique perspective on the world. It can also help us connect with our deepest desires and create a more authentic life. However, this approach can also be challenging because it requires us to step out of our comfort zones and face our fears. It can be easy to get lost in our thoughts and miss what is happening right in front of us. To truly learn from going within, we must be open to what we find there, even if it is uncomfortable or scary.

5. There Is No One Right Path

We can take many different paths in life, and each tradition has its own wisdom to offer. By learning from things that are different from our way, we can get a complete view of the world and find our own way. There is no one right path, but by studying other traditions, we can learn how to live more holistic and fulfilling lives. Each tradition has its way of looking at the world, and by exposure to multiple traditions, we can develop a more nuanced understanding of reality. By learning from different traditions, we can also learn to respect and value the different ways people have lived as we develop our own unique and authentic paths.

6. All Traditions Have Value

There are many ways to learn from traditions. One way is to observe and compare the similarities and differences between our traditions and those of others. By doing this, we can learn more about the value of all traditions and understand them better. Another way to learn from traditions is to take part in them ourselves. This can involve anything from attending religious ceremonies to participating in cultural festivals. Participating in the tradition gives us first-hand knowledge and experience of its meaning and purpose. No matter what method we use, learning from tradition is essential to developing our understanding of the world around us.

7. Respect the Beliefs of Others

Each year, billions of people worldwide celebrate religious and cultural holidays. Though these traditions may differ in many ways, they all share a common purpose: to bring people together. In an increasingly divided world, it is more necessary than ever to respect others' beliefs. One way to do this is to learn about the traditions that they hold dear. By learning about the history and meaning of holidays and traditions, we can better understand how rich our shared humanity is. In addition, we can learn about their values and perspectives when interacting with people from other cultures. Ultimately, embracing diversity can help us build a more compassionate and understanding world.

8. Be Open-Minded and Willing to Learn

One of the best things about traditions is that they can be passed down through generations, giving us a sense of connection to our past. But what if we're not connected to that tradition? Can we still learn from it? *Absolutely!* We can better understand other cultures and customs by being curious and willing to learn. Learning about other traditions can also help us appreciate our heritage. So next time you're presented with an unfamiliar tradition, don't be afraid to give it a try. You might just find that you have a lot to learn from it.

9. Take What Works for You and Leave the Rest

People follow many different traditions, whether it is a religion, culture, or way of life. While some traditions are very old and passed down for generations, others are fairly new and still evolving. Regardless of its age, each tradition has something to offer. The key is to take what works for you and leave the rest. For example, suppose you grew up in a family that always ate dinner together but now live independently. In that case, you might continue that tradition by making sure to sit down for a meal by yourself every night. Or, if you don't like how your workplace operates, you might take inspiration from another company's model and implement some of their practices in your business. Do not be afraid to experiment and find what works best for you. Tradition can be a great source of wisdom and knowledge, but remember that you don't have to follow it blindly. You can cherry-pick the parts that work for you and create your own unique tradition.

10. Have a Sense of Humor

No matter how serious, any tradition can be improved by a sense of humor. This may seem a strange sentiment to have at first since humor is usually seen as the opposite of seriousness and respect. And reverence. However, a healthy dose of humor can help us appreciate the things we hold dear. When we take ourselves too seriously, we can become rigid and inflexible, missing out on the joy that comes from laughter. A sense of humor also allows us to see the world from different perspectives and find common ground. Kabbalah has also influenced hermeticism and the Order of the Golden Dawn. Jewish mystics have long used a set of teachings to figure out what the Hebrew Bible means. Today, people from all walks of life can learn from and appreciate the wisdom of Kabbalah.

There is no single *right way* to learn about and understand the world around us. Most importantly, we are open to learning in whatever way works best for us at any given moment. Sometimes that means looking at the past, and sometimes it means looking within ourselves. The key is to remain open to all possibilities and never to stop learning.

Chapter 2: Can Anyone Become a Kabbalist?

For centuries, Kabbalah was known to be hidden or secret knowledge accessible only to selected individuals who met certain criteria. Initiates into this tradition had to study the Torah and other sacred texts, be male and be at least 40 years old. In recent years, however, these criteria have fallen away, and increasing numbers of rabbis and scholars are making Kabbalah accessible to the masses, regardless of gender, age, or background.

Rabbis and scholars are making Kabbalah accessible to the masses.
https://pixabay.com/es/photos/estrella-de-david-estrella-s%c3%admbolo-458372/

In this chapter, we will explore the changing landscape of Kabbalah and the key concepts that anyone can learn. We will also provide practical advice on how to study this ancient wisdom tradition.

The Changing Scenario of Kabbalah

Kabbalah, which is also called Jewish mysticism, is a group of ancient teachings about how to live a meaningful and happy life. Kabbalah has been passed down through the generations for centuries, providing insight into the nature of God, the universe, and the human soul. In recent years, however, there has been a growing interest in Kabbalah by people of all backgrounds and religious beliefs. This is partly because Kabbalah provides a unique perspective on some of life's most pressing questions, such as "What is the meaning of life?" and "How can I achieve happiness and fulfillment?"

As more and more people seek answers to these questions, Kabbalah is likely to continue to grow in popularity. The good news is that anyone can learn Kabbalah, regardless of age, gender, or religious affiliation. In the past, Kabbalah was passed down orally from teacher to student. Still, nowadays, there are many ways to learn this ancient wisdom tradition— online courses, books, and a plethora of websites.

Many people find that the best way to learn Kabbalah is to find a teacher or mentor who can guide them through the material. Others prefer to study independently, using books, online resources, and courses. Whichever method you choose, the most important thing is to have an open mind and a willingness to learn.

Kabbalah for All

One of the most common misconceptions about Kabbalah is that it is only for certain people, such as rabbis or scholars. Some of the most famous Kabbalists, such as Christian mystics like Meister Eckhart and Teresa of Avila, were not Jewish.

Kabbalah is open to everyone because it is *not a religion*. Rather, it is a *wisdom tradition* that people of any belief system can use. Kabbalah teaches us that there is one God, but this *one God* is not necessarily the same as the God of Judaism, Christianity, or Islam. Instead, Kabbalah teaches that God is a mysterious force humans cannot fully understand. This may sound strange, but it is very freeing. It means you do not need to believe in a specific God to learn and benefit from Kabbalah.

The Criteria for Learning Kabbalah

So, if anyone can learn Kabbalah, what are the criteria for doing so? There are no hard and fast rules; however, a few things will help you understand Kabbalah more effectively. First of all, it is helpful to have some knowledge of Judaism or any other religious tradition. Armed with this kind of knowledge, you will not find the concepts of God and religious rituals strange and difficult to understand. However, it is not essential, and many resources are available to help you learn about Kabbalah.

Another helpful criterion for learning Kabbalah is a willingness to question every life lesson you think you've learned. Kabbalah is not about blindly accepting a set of beliefs. Instead, it is about constantly questioning and probing to gain a deeper understanding of the nature of reality. This can be challenging, but it is also incredibly rewarding!

Finally, it is also helpful to have some prior knowledge of meditation or other forms of introspective work. Kabbalah is very much about working on oneself, so it is helpful to have some experience in this area. However, once again, this is not essential. Many resources can teach you about meditation and other forms of inner work, even if you have no prior experience.

Key Concepts of Kabbalah

Kabbalah includes a system of ethical and spiritual practices designed to help people live in harmony with God and the natural world. Key concepts in Kabbalah include the Tree of Life, the Shekhinah, and Tikkun Olam. The Tree of Life is a symbol of the cosmic order, and it is used to represent the relationship between God and the universe. The Shekhinah is the feminine aspect of God, and Tikkun Olam is the Jewish concept of repairing the world. These concepts offer a way to understand the nature of reality and our place in it. They also guide how we can live our lives in a meaningful and fulfilling way.

1. Ein Sof

One of the key theories in Kabbalah is Ein Sof, which means "the infinite." This concept teaches that God is an infinite being who is beyond all human comprehension. Ein Sof is often represented as a circle with no beginning or end, symbolizing the infinite nature of God. Kabbalists believe that through the study and contemplation of Ein Sof, they can gain insights into the nature of reality and God's purpose for creation. The idea of Ein Sof is used to help people understand that the universe is not limited by what we can see and understand with our five senses. Instead, it is a vast and infinite reality beyond our full comprehension.

2. Sefirot

Sefirot (also spelled "sephiroth"), a series of 10 divine emanations representing different aspects of God, form the heart of Kabbalah. They are often depicted as a tree, with each successive level branching downward from the one above it. Together, they form the framework through which God creates and maintains the universe. The Sefiroth also provide a map for the soul's journey back to God. The Kabbalah belief is that the soul descends into the material world to gain experience and wisdom, and as the soul grows and matures, it begins to yearn for its spiritual source. The sefirot provide a path back to God; through them, the soul can be reunited with its divine source. Understanding and aligning oneself with the sefirot can deepen the connection to the Divine and achieve spiritual enlightenment.

3. Tzimtzum

Tzimtzum is another fundamental concept in Kabbalah. The word Tzimtzum means "contraction" or "withdrawal" and refers to the belief that God withdrew Himself from the world to allow creation to take place. This withdrawal allowed a space to open up in which the world could come into being. The concept of Tzimtzum is used to explain how the physical world came into existence and to describe God's relationship to the world. While Tzimtzum is a complex theological conception, it provides a helpful way of understanding some of the central mysteries of existence.

4. Shekhinah

The Shekhinah is the Divine Presence of God, which is said to dwell within all creation. In Kabbalistic thought, the Shekhinah is often seen as the feminine aspect of God and is sometimes referred to as the "Divine Mother." The Shekhinah is also seen as a powerful force for good, often invoked in prayers and rituals for protection and healing. While the concept of the Shekhinah may be complex, it is central to the Kabbalistic understanding of God and the Universe. The Shekhinah is a reminder that God is present in all things and that the Divine can be found in even the seemingly mundane aspects of life.

5. Tikkun Olam

Tikkun Olam is a Hebrew phrase that means "repair of the world." It is often used to refer to the idea of making the world a better place, and it is also a cornerstone belief t in the Jewish mystical tradition of Kabbalah. The ultimate goal of Tikkun Olam is to restore balance and harmony to the world, and Kabbalists believe this can be achieved through individual acts of kindness and compassion. Kabbalists also teach that we are all connected and that our actions have an impact on the entire world. As such, Tikkun Olam is about improving our lives and working together to create a better world for everyone.

6. The Messiah

In Kabbalah, the Messiah is *not seen* as a single person who will come to save the world. Instead, the Messiah is seen as an energy or force that will repair the world (Tikkun Olam). The coming of the Messiah is often seen as a metaphor for the process of spiritual enlightenment. In other words, the Messiah is not a person but an ideal that we can all strive to achieve. The actuality of the Messiah is central to Kabbalistic thought and provides a powerful way of understanding the ultimate goal of our lives.

7. The World to Come

The *World to Come* is a core tenet of Kabbalah. It refers to the belief that there is a time and place where all will be made right. The World to Come is often seen as a metaphor for heaven or the ultimate goal of our spiritual journey. In Kabbalah, it is believed that the world is constantly evolving and that each generation brings us closer to the World to Come. The concept of the World to Come is a reminder that our journey is not complete and that there is still more work to be done. With this in mind, we can strive to make the world better and bring ourselves closer to the divine.

8. Repentance

Repentance or atonement is another dominant tenet of Judaism and an important part of Kabbalah. Repentance means turning away from sin and returning to God. In Kabbalistic philosophy, it is seen as a powerful tool for spiritual growth. It is believed that we can purify our souls and become closer to God through repentance; it is also a way of asking for forgiveness. This essential part of the Jewish tradition provides a powerful way of understanding our relationship with God.

9. Free Will

Another essential part of the Jewish tradition, *free will* means that we have the power to choose our actions; we are not controlled by fate or destiny. In Kabbalistic thought, it is considered another powerful tool for spiritual growth; through its use, we can make choices that help us to become closer to God. It's also a way of taking responsibility for our own lives, providing a path to a better understanding of our relationship with God.

10. The Torah

The Torah is the central text of Kabbalah and contains a great deal of wisdom and knowledge. It is said that the Torah was revealed to Moses on Mount Sinai and that it contains the secrets of the universe. The Torah is divided into five books: Genesis, Exodus, Leviticus, Numbers, and Deuteronomy – and each book contains different laws and teachings. The Torah also includes the Ten Commandments, which are the basic principles of Kabbalah; understanding its contents is essential for understanding this mystical tradition.

How to Study Kabbalah

While it has been practiced for centuries by rabbis and other Jewish scholars, Kabbalah is not just for experts. The best way to learn Kabbalah is to find a reputable teacher or group to study with; as previously mentioned, many resources are available online and in libraries. Once you have found your best resource(s), read as much as possible about the topic. You may also want to attend workshops or classes taught by experienced practitioners. By immersing yourself in the material, you will gain a deeper understanding of its many important concepts.

Kabbalah can be a complex subject, but it is also incredibly rewarding. Here are some tips to help you get started:

1. Meditation

Kabbalah meditation is one of the main methods used to achieve this connection. During Kabbalah meditation, practitioners focus on a particular Hebrew letter or word. By repeating this letter or word, they focus their mind and open themselves up to divine guidance. As well as providing a deep sense of connection, this practice also helps to promote peace of mind, improve concentration, and reduce stress.

If you're interested in exploring this powerful form of meditation, you should know a few things before getting started. First, find a qualified teacher who can offer guidance and support. Secondly, be prepared for some challenging mental work - Kabbalah meditation is not for everyone. But if you're willing to put in the effort, this can be an incredibly rewarding experience.

2. Reading

Many Kabbalists believe that study is the key to unlocking the universe's secrets. While there are many different ways to study Kabbalah, one of the most essential is *reading*. By engaging with Kabbalistic texts, students begin to develop a deeper understanding of the mystical tradition. However, it is crucial to approach these writings with an open mind and a willingness to explore new ideas. It's not about acquiring knowledge; *it is about transformation.* As such, students should be prepared to question everything they think they know about the world and to view it in a new light. With time and effort, anyone can learn how to study Kabbalah. The journey begins with a simple act of reading.

3. Finding a Teacher

While the roots of Kabbalah date back thousands of years, it is a pearl of timeless wisdom relevant to people of all faiths and backgrounds. If you are interested in studying Kabbalah, consider finding a teacher who resonates with you and your spiritual journey. Many online resources and community groups can help guide you to a qualified teacher in your area. Once you have found him/her, commit to regular study and practice. Kabbalah is not simply a theoretical tradition; it is meant to be applied daily. By studying regularly and putting the principles of Kabbalah into practice, we can create more harmony and balance in our lives.

4. Practice

When we study Kabbalah, we are engaged in the process of self-discovery that can lead to greater clarity, confidence, and peace of mind. The practice of Kabbalah can help us to understand our relationships with others, our place in the world, and our spiritual nature. To get the most out of our studies, approach Kabbalah with an open mind, curiosity, and a willingness to experiment with new ideas. The following are some tips for getting the most out of your Kabbalah studies:

- **Read Widely:** There are many books available on Kabbalah, from introductory texts to more advanced treatises. By reading widely, you will gain a greater understanding of the different aspects of this complex tradition.

- **Study with a Group:** Studying Kabbalah with others can greatly deepen your understanding of the material and connect with like-minded individuals. If you don't have access to a formal study group, consider starting one yourself.

- **Practice What You Learn:** Learning about Kabbalah is only useful if you apply what you learn in your everyday life. Experiment with meditation and visualization techniques to see how they affect your thoughts, emotions, and behavior.

By following these tips, you can make the most out of your Kabbalah studies and reap the benefits of this ancient wisdom tradition.

5. Community

At its core are personal growth and spiritual evolution. Kabbalah teaches that we are all connected and that our actions impact others. Finding a community of like-minded individuals who can offer support and guidance is crucial, and again, online resources and local groups are your best bet. Find a teacher or guide who can offer personalized instruction and help you find your study path.

6. Service

A great way to Kabbalah is to offer service to others. When we give of ourselves without expectation of anything in return, we open our hearts and minds to new possibilities. We also come to understand that, as interconnected beings, our personal growth ultimately benefits the entire world. The following are some ways you can offer service to others:

- **Volunteer Your Time:** Many organizations could benefit from your time and energy. Consider volunteering at a local soup kitchen, Habitat for Humanity, or any other organization that speaks to you.

- **Donate Money:** If you are unable or unwilling to volunteer your time, consider making a financial contribution to a worthy cause.

- **Help a Friend:** Sometimes, the best way to help others is simply to be there for them. If you have a friend who is going through a tough time, offer your support. Listen to them, offer advice if asked, and just be a shoulder to cry on.

- **Be Kind:** One of the simplest and most effective ways to serve others is to simply be kind. Smile at strangers, hold the door open for someone, or just take the time to converse with someone. These small acts of kindness can make a big difference in the world.

By offering service to others, we make the world a better place and open ourselves up to new possibilities and experiences.

Kabbalah is an ancient wisdom tradition that offers a unique perspective on the nature of reality. It is a complex system of thought that can be difficult to understand, but the rewards of study are well worth the effort. Kabbalah can help us to understand our place in the world and to see the interconnectedness of all things. It also provides a framework for personal growth and spiritual evolution. Finding a community of like-minded individuals who can offer support and guidance is important to get the most out of your studies.

And finally, remember that one of the best ways to learn Kabbalah is to offer service to others. By following these tips, you can make the most out of your studies and reap the many benefits of this ancient wisdom tradition.

Chapter 3: One Tree, Seven Chakras, and Four Worlds

Kabbalah teaches us that there is a spiritual dimension to reality and that we can tap into this dimension to experience a more profound sense of meaning and purpose in our lives. Through the process of Kabbalah, we can learn to connect with this spiritual realm and use its power to create change in our lives; it provides a way to understand and work with the spiritual forces that are all around us.

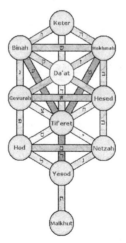

The Tree of Life is one of the foremost symbols in Kabbalah.
https://commons.wikimedia.org/wiki/File:Ktreewnames.png

The Tree of Life is a key principle in Kabbalah. This chapter will give an overview of the Tree of Life and how it is used to explain both the big and small picture. We will also examine the links between the Tree of Life, sacred geometry, and the Hindu and Buddhist traditions' seven main chakras. By understanding these concepts, we can begin to tap into the spiritual power of Kabbalah.

The Kabbalistic Tree of Life

The Tree of Life is one of the foremost symbols in Kabbalah, which is a Jewish mystical tradition. The tree is made up of 10 spheres, called *sephiroth*, each showing a different part of God. These spheres are connected by 22 paths, representing the soul's journey as it ascends to Godhood. The Tree of Life is a map of reality, and its sephiroth and courses offer a way to understand the divine nature of Creation. People also believe that a tree is a powerful tool for meditation and thinking. Visualizing the tree can teach you a lot about reality and your place in it.

The Tree of Life has been an important part of the Kabbalah for hundreds of years, and anyone who wants to learn from it can still do so. The tree can be used as a tool for meditation and contemplation. Traditionally, Kabbalists would sit with the tree in front of them and focus their attention on each individual sephirah. As they did so, they would meditate on the qualities of that sephirah and how they related to their own lives. In this way, the tree could be used as a tool for self-discovery and growth.

The Tree's Role in Describing the Macrocosm and the Microcosm

The tree is important because it can represent both the big (macro) and small (micro) picture; the macrocosm is the universe as a whole, and the microcosm is the individual human being. The tree can be seen as a map of reality, with each sephirah representing a different aspect of the universe. It can also be seen as a model of the human psyche, with each sephirah representing a different side of the self.

The tree is also significant because it shows the *relationship between* the macrocosm and the microcosm. Kabbalists use the Tree of Life (the sephirot diagram) to figure out what God is like and how the universe works. The tree is often shown as a person's body, with the head standing for God, the trunk for the world that God made, and the branches for the different levels of reality. The Tree of Life is an ancient symbol used by numerous cultures throughout history. The Tree of Life is a powerful symbol of life. It is often shown as a big tree with branches reaching up to the sky and roots deep into the ground.

In addition to being a map of reality, it is also an important way to explain how the big and small picture fit together. The branches represent the heavens, while the roots represent the underworld. The tree trunk, which connects the two, symbolizes the journey between these two realms. This journey is known as the "Middle Way," which is believed to be the key to achieving balance in one's life.

The Tree of Life is also often used to symbolize the human body. In this comparison, the tree's head stands for God, the trunk for the human body, and the branches for the different levels of reality. Just as the tree has roots that extend into the ground, so does the human body have roots (the feet) connecting it to the earth. And just as the tree has branches that reach up to the sky, so does the human body have branches (arms) extending out into the world.

Kabbalistic teaching says that the universe is a reflection of God and that each level of reality is like a different part of God. The Sephiroth, or spheres of the tree, symbolize these different aspects, and the paths connecting them represent the soul's journey as it ascends to Godhood. In other words, the Tree of Life is a map of reality, and its sephiroth and paths offer a way to understand the divine nature of Creation.

The tree is a powerful symbol of life, and its wisdom can be used to understand both the macrocosm and the microcosm. By understanding the tree, we can begin to understand the nature of reality and our place within it.

The Connections between the Tree and the Sacred Geometry

The *Tree of Life* is often used in conjunction with other symbols, such as the *Flower of Life* and the *Seed of Life*. These symbols are all based on sacred geometry, which is the study of the patterns found in nature. Sacred geometry is used to understand the relationship between the physical and spiritual worlds.

The Flower of Life is a symbol that consists of overlapping circles. It is said to represent the cycle of life, death, and rebirth.

The Seed of Life is a symbol that consists of seven overlapping circles. It is said to represent the seven days of creation, and it is often used in conjunction with the Tree of Life.

The Tree of Life and the Flower of Life are both based on the Fibonacci sequence. In the Fibonacci sequence, each number is the sum of the two numbers that came before it. The Fibonacci sequence begins with 0 and 1 and goes on to infinity. The relationship between the Tree of Life and the Fibonacci sequence is simple - each sephira on the Tree of Life corresponds to a number in the Fibonacci sequence.

The first sephira, Kether, corresponds to the number 0, while the second sephira, Chokmah, corresponds to the number 1. The third sephira, Binah, corresponds to the number 2, and so on. This relationship between the Tree of Life and the Fibonacci sequence is known as the "Fibonacci Code." The Fibonacci Code is a way of understanding the relationship between the physical and spiritual worlds. It is based on the idea that everything in the universe is connected – and there is a pattern to this connection.

The Tree of Life can be used to understand the Fibonacci Code. By understanding the symbolism of the Tree of Life, we can understand the patterns found in nature.

The Tree of Life and the Chakras

The Tree of Life is also often used in conjunction with the chakras. The chakras are energy centers in the human body that are said to be responsible for our physical, mental, and emotional health. There are seven main chakras, each associated with a different sephira on the Tree of Life.

The first chakra, the root chakra, is located at the base of the spine. It is associated with sephira Malkuth. The second chakra, the sacral chakra, is located in the lower abdomen. It is associated with the sephira Yesod. The third chakra, the solar plexus chakra, is located in the upper abdomen. It is associated with the sephira Hod.

The fourth chakra, the heart chakra, is found in the center of the chest. It is associated with the sephira Tiphereth. The fifth chakra, the throat chakra, is in the throat. It is associated with the sephira Netzach. The sixth chakra, known as the third eye chakra, is located in between the eyebrows. It is associated with the sephira Hod. The seventh chakra, the crown chakra, is at the top of the head. It is associated with the sephira Kether.

In Hinduism, the chakras are said to be responsible for our physical, mental, and emotional health. Buddhism also knows how important the chakras are, and people often use them when they meditate. The chakras can be used to understand the Tree of Life. By understanding the relationship between the chakras and the Tree of Life, we can understand the connection between the physical and spiritual worlds.

The Four Kabbalistic Worlds

There are four holistic worlds, each with its unique energy and purpose.

The *first world* is called Atzilut, and it is the world of *pure spirit*. It is the highest and most rarefied of the four worlds and is where God resides. Also known as the world of archetypes, this is the world of pure ideas, where everything is perfect and unified.

The **second world** is called Beriyah, the world of Creation. It is here that the physical universe comes into existence. This is the world of form, where things take shape and begin to interact with each other.

The **third world** is called Yetzirah, the world of formation. It is here that the energy of Creation takes form and substance. This is the world of action and reaction, where things come into being and interact with each other.

The **fourth and final world** is called Assiah, and it is the world of action. It is here that our thoughts and deeds take shape in the physical world. This is the world of manifestation, where things exist in time and space.

Each of these four worlds has an important role in spiritual development. To grow spiritually, we must first connect with the world of pure spirit (Atzilut). From there can begin to create our reality in the world of Creation (Briah). Once we have created our reality, we can begin to give it form and substance in the world of formation (Yetzirah). Finally, we can bring our thoughts and deeds into physical manifestation in the world of action (Assiah). The Tree of Life is a map that helps us understand the relationship between these four worlds. It is a useful tool for anyone who wants to learn more about life's mysteries.

1. Atziluth

Atziluth is the highest of the four worlds in Kabbalistic thought. It is the world of divine emanation, where God's light and love first flow forth. This is the realm of pure spirit, where all is unity, and there is no duality or division. From Atziluth comes the light that illuminates all the other worlds. In Jewish tradition, Atziluth is often called the World to Come because it is the source of all blessings and perfections. Those who dwell in Atziluth are said to be close to God, and they enjoy a state of perpetual bliss.

The name *Atziluth* comes from a Hebrew root that means "to go forth." This means that Atziluth is the world from which all others come. It is also sometimes called the World of Emanations because it is where divine energies first flow forth. In Kabbalah, ten sefirot, or divine emanations, represent different aspects of God's nature. These Sefirot begin in Atziluth and flow down into the other threads. Each sefirah has its own characteristic energy and color. Together, they all make up a reality map showing how everything in creation is interconnected, which is what the Tree of Life means. Everything originates from Atziluth and flows down through the other worlds before returning to its source.

Those who dwell in Atziluth are said to be close to God and enjoy a state of permanent bliss. This world is often described as a place of great light and beauty. In Kabbalistic writing, Atziluth is often compared to the material world, which is seen as a dark and distorted reflection of the real world. The things we see in this world are only shadows of their true counterparts in Atziluth. But even though our world isn't a perfect copy of Atziluth, there are still bits of divine light in it. By studying Kabbalah and meditating on the nature of reality, we can glimpse Atziluth and experience some of its peace and bliss in our lives.

2. Briah

The Kabbalistic world of Briah is a realm of pure thought and potential. It is the world of the divine architect, of unformed matter awaiting the shaping hand of God. In Briah, everything is possible, and nothing is concrete. It is a world of infinite potential and limitless possibility.

The Kabbalists teach that Briah is the world that we create through our thoughts and actions. Every thought and every deed brings into existence a new reality. This is why it is so important to be mindful of our thoughts and actions, for they have the power to shape our world. The Kabbalists also teach that we have the power to choose which reality we want to create. We can choose love or fear, harmony or discord, light or darkness. The choice is ours.

Briah is also the world of miracles. In Briah, all things are possible, and so miracles are commonplace. Miracles are not violations of natural law; they are simply manifestations of the unlimited power of God. If we open our hearts and minds to the possibility of miracles, they will surely come into our lives.

The Kabbalistic world of Briah is a realm of boundless potential and limitless possibility. It is a world that we create through our thoughts and actions. And it is a world where miracles are commonplace. What more could we ask for?

3. Yetzirah

Yetzirah is the third of the four Kabbalistic worlds, and it is sometimes referred to as the world of formation. In this world, the Divine light is clothed in various forms, giving rise to all of the manifold creaturely life that we see around us. While our physical world is Yetzirah's lowest manifestation, it is by no means the only one. The spiritual realms above us are also part of Yetzirah, and each has its unique form and character. Just as we ascend from the physical to the mental and spiritual realms, so can we descend from Yetzirah into the lower worlds. By doing so, we can gain a deeper understanding of the nature of reality and our place within it.

4. Assiah

In the Kabbalistic tradition, each world is a more spiritual level of reality, with Assiah being the most physical and Atzilut being the most spiritual. Even though we live in all four worlds every day, most of us don't know about the higher levels of reality that exist above the physical world. Kabbalists believe that it is our task in life to raise our consciousness to these higher levels to bring more spirituality into our lives and help create a better world. By gaining a better understanding of the Kabbalistic concept of Assiah, we can begin to see the world around us in a new light and open ourselves up to a deeper level of understanding.

Kabbalah is a mystical tradition that teaches about the nature of reality and our place within it. It is a system of thought that can help us understand the world and our place within it. Kabbalah can also help us connect with our higher selves and the Divine. Kabbalah is a tradition open to everyone, regardless of religious affiliation.

The Tree of Life is a central symbol in Kabbalah, and it can be used to understand the nature of reality and our place within it. The connection between the chakras and the Tree of Life helps us understand the relationship between our physical bodies and spiritual selves. The chakras are energy centers that run along the spine from the base to the crown. They are connected to the body's major organs and represent different aspects of our being, and each chakra is associated with a different level of reality. They can be used to understand the nature of reality and our place within it.

The Tree of Life is divided into four worlds, each representing a different level of reality. The Kabbalistic tradition teaches us that there are four levels of reality, each progressively more spiritual than the last. The physical world is Assiah, the world of action. The mental world is Yetzirah, the world of formation. The spiritual world is Briah, the world of creation, and the divine world is Atzilut, the world of emanation. Even though we live in all four worlds every day, most of us don't know about the higher levels of reality that exist above the physical world. Kabbalists believe that it is our task in life to raise our consciousness to these higher levels to bring more spirituality into our lives and help create a better world.

Chapter 4: The Sephirot I. The Supernal Triad

The Kabbalistic Tree of Life is composed of 10 spiritual principles or Sephirot. The first three sephiroth are called the supernal triad, symbolizing the highest level of spirituality a human can attain. The supernal triad comprises Kether, Chokmah, and Binah. In the previous chapter, we introduced the concept of the Kabbalistic tree of life and explained what a sephirah is.

The first three sephiroth are called the supernal triad.
Edaina, CC BY-SA 3.0 <http://creativecommons.org/licenses/by-sa/3.0/>, via Wikimedia Commons: https://commons.wikimedia.org/wiki/File:The_one_tr%C3%A4d.jpg

The Sephirot are the 10 divine emanations of God, and each one corresponds to a different side of the human experience. In this chapter, we will focus on the first three sephirot, known as the Supernal Triad. These sephirot correspond to the highest level of reality, known as the world of Atziluth.

Kether is the first sephirah, and it symbolizes the divine principle. It is the highest level of spirituality that a human can attain. Chokmah is the second sephirah, and it symbolizes wisdom. Binah is the third sephirah, and it symbolizes understanding.

The supernal triad is often represented as a triangle, with Kether at the top, Chokmah in the middle, and Binah at the bottom. This is because the three sephirot are considered to be interrelated and mutually supportive. Each sephirah has its unique qualities, but they all work together to create a harmonious whole. In this chapter, we will explore the individual qualities of each sephirah in the supernal triad.

The Supernal Triad

The Supernal Triad is one of the key concepts in Kabbalah. This is the belief that there are three levels of reality: the physical world, the spiritual world, and the divine world. Each level has its laws and principles. The physical world is governed by the laws of physics; the spiritual world is governed by the laws of karma, and the divine world by the will of God. Kabbalists believe that we can access all three levels of reality through our thoughts, words, and actions. By aligning our lives with the highest level of reality, we create positive change in ourselves and the world around us.

The Supernal Triad comprises three sephirot: Kether, Binah, and Chokmah. Each of these sephirot corresponds to a different Pillar of Reality. The Pillar of Severity represents Kether, the first sephirah; the Pillar of Mercy represents Binah, the second sephirah; and the Pillar of Balance represents Chokmah, the third sephirah. The three Pillars of Reality are the foundation upon which all of existence is built. To understand the nature of reality, we must first understand the nature of these three Pillars.

Each sephirah in the Supernal Triad is composed of the other two sephirot. For example, Kether is composed of Binah and Chokmah, Binah is composed of Kether and Chokmah, and Chokmah is composed of Kether and Binah. This is because each sephirah contains the energy of the other two sephirot. The Supernal Triad is, therefore, a microcosm of the entire tree of life, the highest level of reality, and it contains all of the other sephirot within it.

The Structure of the Triad

The Supernal Triad is structured in a particular way. The first sephirah, Kether, is masculine; the second sephirah, Binah, is feminine; and the third sephirah, Chokmah, is balanced. This structure reflects the duality of existence. Kabbalah teaches that everything in the universe is composed of two opposing forces: male and female, light and dark, good and evil. This duality is necessary for existence. Without it, there would be no motion, change, or life.

The Supernal Triad also reflects the trinity of existence. Kabbalah teaches that there are three elements to every experience: mind, body, and spirit. Every thought, every feeling, and every action has a mental, physical, and spiritual component. This trinity is necessary for existence. Without it, we would not be able to understand or experience reality.

The Supernal Triad is the foundation of the Tree of Life. It is the blueprint for existence. Everything that exists in the universe is a reflection of the Supernal Triad. By understanding the nature of the Supernal Triad, we can begin to understand the nature of reality.

The supernal triad is considered to be the highest level of spirituality because it represents the purest form of divine energy. This is the level where we can commune with God directly, without the interference of the material world. When we reach this level, we will directly understand the divine principle.

The supernal triad also forms the base for all other sephirot. Just as a house cannot stand without a strong foundation, the other sephirot cannot exist without the support of the supernal triad. If you are interested in reaching the supernal triad, it is crucial to understand the nature of each sephirah. In the next section, we will look closely at each sephirah in the supernal triad and explore its unique qualities.

Kether - The Pillar of Severity

Kether is the first Sephiroth on the Tree of Life, representing pure Spirit. It is considered the highest point on the Tree, and the crown symbolizes it. In some treatments, Kether is also known as the Ain Soph or the limitless light. Echoing this idea of limitlessness, Kether is often said to be both formless and devoid of any qualities. It might be tough to comprehend at first, but remember that Kether is also the origin of all Manifestations. Everything that exists stems from Kether, which means it contains the potential for everything. Even though it may seem formless and without qualities, Kether is still the source of all Creation - an important distinction to remember.

Relation to Divinity

Kether is the closest sephirah to the divine realm. It is said to be the first spark of creation and contains the potential for all other sephirot. Kabbalists believe that we can access the divine realm through Kether. By meditating on Kether, we can connect with the highest level of reality and tap into God's infinite wisdom and power.

Kether, also known as the Crown, sits at the top of the tree, above all the other sephirah, representing unity and pure divine energy. Every sephira is a part of Kether and is present in all things. Kether is often seen as a symbol of God or the Divine Mind. It is infinite and unchanging, and it represents our highest potential. We all aspire to reach the level of unity and wholeness that Kether represents. When we do, we will find that we are truly connected to the Divine.

Exercise

There are many ways to connect with Kether. One is to meditate on the sephirah. Sit in a comfortable position and close your eyes. Visualize a bright, white light above you. See this light growing larger and brighter until it surrounds you. This is the energy of Kether. Feel the energy of Kether flowing through you. Experience the unity and wholeness that it represents. Allow yourself to be filled with the light of Kether.

Another exercise is to think about a time when you felt connected to something greater than yourself. It could be a religious or spiritual experience or simply a moment when you felt a deep sense of peace and connection. What did that experience feel like? How did it change your perspective on life? Spend some time writing about that experience and what it meant to you. Then, reflect on how you can bring that feeling into your everyday life. What small steps can you take to help you feel more connected to the Divine?

Binah - The Pillar of Mercy

Binah is the second sephirah on the Tree of Life and represents understanding. The yin-yang symbol symbolizes it and is often referred to as the Great Mother. Binah is considered to be the feminine aspect of God and is said to be the source of all manifestation. It is her role to bring forth life from the womb of potentiality. In the same way, Binah is responsible for giving birth to our ideas and plans. She is the archetype of the great Cosmic Mother who brings new life into existence. Binah is often seen as a symbol of wisdom; we can understand the world around us through Binah. Without Binah, there would be no creation.

Binah is also known as the Pillar of Mercy because she is the one who bestows compassion and pardon upon us. She helps us to see the good in others, even when they have done wrong. Binah teaches us to forgive and reminds us that we are all connected in the web of life. When we show mercy to others, we are showing mercy to ourselves. Binah is the realm of pure love; we can receive divine guidance and wisdom through her grace.

Masculine and Feminine Aspects

In the Kabbalistic tradition, Binah is often represented by the color black; her symbol is the yin-yang. Binah is the mother of all the other sephirot and is seen as the embodiment of compassion and wisdom. Her chief characteristic is mercy. Binah also has a masculine aspect known as Chokhmah. Chokhmah is associated with the color white, and his symbol is the sun. Chokhmah is considered to be the father of all the sephirot, and he represents willpower and intelligence. He is also known for his justice and can be very stern when necessary. Together, these two aspects of Binah help to create a balanced universe.

Relation to Chokmah

Binah is traditionally seen as being in a relationship of receptivity to Chokmah, the second sephira, and the Masculine Divine. In other words, Binah receives creative energy from Chokmah and gives birth to manifestation. Binah is also seen as the Great Mother, giving form to Chokmah's energy through her womb. She is often seen as a dark or shadowy figure because she is also associated with the Underground World, where new life is formed. Binah is a powerful and necessary part of Creation, without which manifestation would not be possible.

Exercise

Meditating on Binah can help us to connect with our feminine energy and wisdom. It can also help us understand receptivity's role in manifestation. Spend some time in meditation, visualizing yourself as Binah. Allow yourself to receive the creative energy of the Universe and give birth to your deepest desires. Ask Binah to show you the way to compassion and wisdom, and allow her to fill you with her love and mercy.

When you are ready, close your eyes and begin to breathe deeply. Allow your mind to become still and focused. Imagine a column of white light descending from the heavens and entering through the top of your head. This is the light of Chokmah, the father principle. Feel this light enter your being and fill you with its radiant energy. Now imagine a column of black light rising from the earth and entering through the bottom of your feet. This is the light of Binah, the mother principle. Feel this light enter your being and fill you with its loving energy.

Allow these two lights to meet in the middle of your body, and feel their energies merge. You begin to feel a sense of balance and harmony as they merge. Allow yourself to be filled with the light of Binah and Chokmah. Feel their love and wisdom enter your being. Allow yourself to receive their guidance and direction. When you are ready, open your eyes and allow yourself to return to the present moment.

Take some time to journal about your experience. What did you see? What did you feel? What guidance did Binah and Chokmah offer you? Allow their wisdom to guide you in your life from this day forward.

Chokmah - The Pillar of Balance

Chokmah, the second sephirah, is known as the pillar of balance. It represents the masculine principle of creation and is associated with the element of air. The goal of Chokmah is to achieve a balance between the extremes of form and formlessness. This is symbolized by the image of a scale, with one side representing form and the other side representing formlessness. To achieve balance, Chokmah must find the middle between these two extremes. By doing so, it helps to bring harmony to the universe.

Chokmah is considered to be the first sephirah because it is the source of all creative energy. Chokmah is associated with the color white, and its symbol is the sun. The sun is seen as a symbol of life-giving energy, representing the power of Chokmah to create and sustain life.

Chokmah is a powerful sephirah, and all of the other sephirot feel its energy. It is the source of all creative power, and it is from this power that manifestation occurs. Chokmah is also associated with wisdom. Wisdom is the ability to see things from a higher perspective and understand reality's true nature. It is the knowledge that comes from understanding the relationships between all things.

Wisdom is a necessary part of the balance; it is through it that Chokmah brings harmony to the universe. By understanding the true nature of reality, Chokmah can see the relationships between all things. This understanding allows Chokmah to find the middle way between the extremes of form and formlessness. In this way, Chokmah brings balance to the universe.

Relation to Binah and Kether

Chokmah, the second sephira on the Tree of Life, is considered to be the "Father" principle. It is associated with the element of air and the colors white and silver. Chokmah is positioned opposite Binah on the Tree, and together they form the "Supernal Triangle." Above them is Kether, the first sephira. While Chokmah is considered very active and dynamic, Binah is more passive and receptive.

Together, these three sephirot represent the beginning of Creation. Kether is the point of origin, while Chokmah and Binah represent the first two stages of manifestation. In some ways, they can be thought of as the "Big Bang," followed by the universe's expansion. Together, these three sephirot embody the creative power of God.

Active Imagination Exercise

One way to connect with the energy of Chokmah is through active imagination. This is a process where you use your imagination to connect with the divine. To begin, find a quiet place where you will not be disturbed. Close your eyes and take several deep breaths. Then, allow your mind to wander. Visualize yourself walking through a beautiful garden. Notice the colors, smells, and textures around you.

As you explore, you come across a door. Open the door and step into a new world. What do you see? Spend some time exploring this new place. When you are ready, return to the present moment and take a few minutes to journal about your experience. An active imagination is a powerful tool for connecting with the sephirah of Chokmah. You can access hidden wisdom and bring creative ideas to life by exploring your inner world.

Da'at - The Hidden Sephirah

In the Kabbalistic tradition, there is a concept known as Da'at, which refers to hidden knowledge or wisdom. This hidden sephirah is said to be located at the center of the Tree of Life and is thought to be the source of all understanding. While the other sephirah can be studied and understood through traditional methods, Da'at is said to be beyond such means. It can only be accessed through direct experience, and this direct knowledge is said to lead to true enlightenment. In many ways, Da'at represents the ultimate goal of the Kabbalistic journey. It is where all understanding comes together, and it is from here that we can see the entire Tree of Life in its true form.

Connection to the Other Sephirot

Da'at is the final of the ten sephirot on the Kabbalistic Tree of Life, and it is thought to represent knowledge or understanding. Da'at is often depicted as a point of connection between the other sephirot and is seen as the place where all the different energies come together. In some ways, Da'at can be seen as the ultimate goal of the Tree of Life, representing a state of harmony and balance between all the different parts of the self. To reach Da'at, one must first go through a process of coming to know and understand oneself and then learn to see the same truths in others. Only when we have developed a deep connection to the other sephirot can we hope to attain Da'at.

Meditation Exercise

One way to connect with the energy of Da'at is through meditation. This is a process of quieting the mind and opening up to the flow of universal knowledge. To begin, find a comfortable place to sit or lie down. Close your eyes and take several deep breaths. Then, allow your mind to become still. Simply observe the thoughts and sensations that pass through your consciousness. Do not judge or analyze what you experience; simply let it be.

After a while, you may find that you enter into a state of deep peace and understanding. This is the energy of Da'at, and it is from here that true wisdom arises. Spend some time exploring this state of consciousness. When you are ready, return to the present moment and take a few minutes to journal about your experience. Meditation is a powerful tool for connecting with the sephirah of Da'at. By quieting the mind, you can access the hidden wisdom of the universe and bring greater understanding into your life.

The sephirot are best understood as a map of consciousness that can be used to navigate the inner landscape of the psyche. Each sephirah represents a different aspect of the self. By exploring these different energies, we can better understand who we are and what we are capable of. The sephirot can also be used as a tool for personal transformation. By working with the different energies represented by the sephirah, we can learn to create balance and harmony within ourselves and, in turn, bring more peace and happiness into our lives.

This chapter has introduced the concept of the sephirot and explored the first three sephiroth of the Tree of Life. In the next chapters, we will continue our journey down the Tree of Life and explore the remaining seven sephiroth. We will also learn about the mystical practice of Kabbalah and how it can be used to bring greater understanding and insight into our lives.

Chapter 5: The Sephirot II: The Ethical Triad

In the last chapter, we began to explore the symbolism of the sephirot – or the 10 divine emanations of God. We started with the top three sephirot on the Tree of Life, which belong to the world of Atzilut: Keter, Chokhmah, and Binah. In this chapter, we will move lower on the Tree of Life and explore the next trifecta of sephirot, which belongs to the world of Briah: Gevurah, Chesed, and Tiferet.

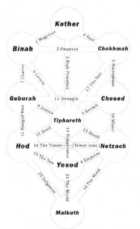

The three sephirot of the ethical triad are Gevurah, Chesed, and Tiferet.
Alan SyncBookPress, CC BY-SA 3.0 <https://creativecommons.org/licenses/by-sa/3.0>, via Wikimedia Commons: https://commons.wikimedia.org/wiki/File:Tree_of_Life_Tarot.jpg

This next group of sephirot is often called the "ethical triad" because they represent the three most important parts of ethical behavior: power, love, and beauty. Just as the previous sephirot represented different aspects of God, these sephirot also represented different aspects of the human soul. We will explore each sephirah in turn and see how we can use the symbolism of these divine emanations to help us lead more balanced and fulfilling lives.

The Ethical Triad

The three sephirot of the ethical triad are Gevurah, Chesed, and Tiferet. Gevurah is associated with power, Chesed with love, and Tiferet with beauty. These sephirot are arranged in a particular order on the Tree of Life. Gevurah is on the left, Chesed is on the right, and Tiferet is in the middle. This arrangement is significant because it shows the relationship between these sephirot. Gevurah and Chesed are opposite, just as power and love are opposite forces. Tiferet is in the middle because it is the synthesis of these two opposites. The balance between power and love is the essence of beauty.

This triad of sephirot also represents the three fundamental aspects of ethical behavior. Gevurah represents the ability to restrain oneself, Chesed represents the ability to give, and Tiferet represents the ability to find a middle way between these two extremes. These three sephirot teach us that the key to ethical behavior is balance. We must learn to restrain our power, so it does not become destructive, and we must learn to give of ourselves without becoming self-sacrificial. Only when we find this balance will we be able to act beautifully and ethically.

This triad is a three-part framework that can be used to evaluate ethical systems. It consists of three components: deontology, consequentialism, and virtue ethics. Deontology is the view that ethics is about duty and principle and that the right thing to do is determined by considering one's obligations. Consequentialism, on the other hand, is the view that the right thing to do is determined by considering the consequences of one's actions. Virtue ethics, finally, is the view that ethics is about developing character traits that enable one to live a good life.

Each of these points of view has its pros and cons, but they can be put together to make a stronger moral system. The Sephirot guides you towards a helpful way of thinking about these different ethics and how they relate to each other. These spheres belong to the Kabbalistic world of Briah. Gevurah is the masculine sephirah, Chesed is the feminine sephirah, and Tiferet is the child of these two opposites. In the following section, we will explore each sephirah in turn and see how they can help us create a more balanced and ethical life.

Gevurah: Power

The ethical triad comprises three sephirot, which are different aspects of God. The first, Gevurah, represents power. This sephirah is often linked to strictness and judgment because it shows the ability to set limits and control yourself. Gevurah is the quality of strength or severity. It is the ability to restrain oneself, to hold back, and be disciplined.

This sephirah is necessary for us to live a balanced and ethical life. Without Gevurah, we would be prone to excess and indulgence. We would have no self-control and no ability to set boundaries. We would be like children, acting on our instincts without any thought to the consequences of our actions. But Gevurah is not just about self-control. It is also about using our power wisely. This sephirah teaches us that we must use our power for good, not for evil. We must use our power to help others, not to harm them. And we must use our power to create, not to destroy.

Masculine Principle

In Jewish mysticism, Gevurah is the masculine principle, representing strength, discipline, and judgment. It is often compared to the Greek god Ares or the Roman god Mars. In the Kabbalah, Gevurah is associated with the fifth sefira, called Din or Judgment. It is also known as the "Left Hand of God." The feminine principle, Binah or Understanding, is represented by the right hand of God. Together, these two sefirot represent balance and harmony. While Gevurah represents the power to destroy, Binah represents the power to create. Without both of these forces, the universe would be in chaos.

The Force of Limitation

In the Jewish mystical tradition, Gevurah is the principle of judgment and limitation. It is the power that sets boundaries and establishes order. Without Gevurah, the world would be in chaos. This force is symbolized by the color black, and it is associated with the element of fire. When we work with Gevurah energy, we align ourselves with the divine will and learn to trust in a higher power. We are also working to cultivate strength and discipline. By learning to control our energy, we can create meaningful change in our lives and the world around us.

The Power to Discern Good and Evil

In the Hebrew faith, Gevurah is the fifth sephirah or divine attribute. It is associated with justice, discipline, and the power to discern good from evil. Gevurah is often represented by a sword, which indicates its power to cut through lies and illusions. The followers of this faith believe that all have the power to discern right from wrong but that this power must be used wisely. We must learn to control our energy and use it for good, not evil. When we are faced with a difficult decision, it is through Gevurah that we can clearly see what is right and what is wrong. In this way, Gevurah helps us to maintain our integrity and live lives of honesty and truth.

The Quality of Justice

Gevurah is most often translated as "severity" or "strength," but it can also mean "justice." Justice is not always easy. It requires us to stand up for what is right, even when it is difficult or unpopular. It means being fair and unbiased and treating others with respect. Gevurah reminds us that justice is an essential aspect of a healthy society. Justice is not always easy, but it is always worth striving for. Gevurah reminds us of the importance of pursuing justice, even when it is hard. By doing so, we create a fairer world and justice for all.

Unlocking the Power of Gevurah

There are many ways to unlock the power of Gevurah in your life. One is to learn to control your energy. You can do this through practices like meditation, yoga, and breathwork. By learning to control your energy, you will become more aware of the energy around you and how it affects you. You will also be better able to use your energy for good.

Working on getting stronger and more disciplined is another way to open up the power of Gevurah. Martial arts, weightlifting, or any other activity that requires focus and discipline are excellent practices to awaken your power. By working on these things, you will develop the strength and discipline you need to stand up for what is right and to make meaningful changes in your life.

Lastly, you can also use Gevurah's power by learning about the teachings of the Hebrew faith. By understanding the principles of this faith, you will be better able to see what is right and wrong. You will also be better equipped to live a life of honesty and truth.

Chesed - The Power of Love

Chesed is the sphere of mercy in the ethical triad. It is associated with the element of water and the color blue. Chesed is the force that binds us together and allows us to feel compassion for others. It is through Chesed that we can give and receive love. In the Jewish mystical tradition, Chesed is the principle of love and compassion. The power brings us together and allows us to feel empathy for others.

Without Chesed, the world would be a cold and lonely place. When we work with Chesed energy, we are opening our hearts to love and compassion. We are also working to cultivate kindness and generosity. We can create a more loving and compassionate world by learning to give and receive love.

Feminine Principle

According to Jewish tradition, Chesed, which means "loving-kindness," is the highest and most important way to give. It is often linked to the feminine principle because it has qualities like mercy, compassion, and grace. Chesed is not simply a matter of performing acts of charity; rather, it is a way of being that stems from a deep inner wellspring of love and compassion. When we act from a place of Chesed, we do so without expectations or ulterior motives; we give simply because it is in our nature to do so. We may not always be aware of it, but every act of Chesed has the power to change our lives and the world around us for the better.

The Force of Expansion

In Judaism, the concept of Chesed is often translated as "loving-kindness." However, Chesed encompasses a much broader range of meanings than simply an act of kindness. The rabbis say Chesed helps us see beyond our own points of view and reach a place where we can understand and care about others.

In the Talmud, it is written that "the whole world is sustained by the merit of Chesed." This teaches us that acts of kindness are not only consequential in terms of our relationships, but they also have the power to positively impact the world at large. When we expand our loving-kindness to include all beings, we help create a more harmonious and whole world.

The Power of Love and Compassion

The Hebrew word Chesed also includes the ideas of compassion, goodwill, and loyalty, and it is often described as an act of mercy. It lies at the heart of many religious traditions. In the Jewish faith, the Talmud teaches us that Chesed should be extended not only to fellow Jews but to all human beings, regardless of race or religion.

Chesed also forms the basis for many acts of charity and altruism. By definition, it requires putting others before ourselves and acting with their best interests at heart. In a world that can sometimes seem driven by selfishness and greed, Chesed reminds us of the importance of love and compassion. Ultimately, Chesed is about creating a more just and caring world for all.

The Quality of Mercy

Chesed is often associated with compassion, love, and giving, representing how we express our love for others. It is the foundation of all human relationships and allows us to see the good in others even when they make mistakes. Chesed reminds us that everyone deserves to be treated with respect and understanding, and it gives us the strength to forgive. Chesed is not simply an emotion; it is an active choice to be loyal and faithful, even when it is difficult. It is a decision to show mercy, even when we do not feel like it. As we learn to show mercy towards others, we open ourselves up to receiving God's infinite mercy. In turn, this helps us to create a more compassionate world.

Unlocking the Power of Chesed

Chesed is a way of being that requires us to put others before ourselves and act with their best interests at heart. It is a quality of mercy and compassion that can improve our lives and the world around us. When we choose to extend Chesed to all beings, we help to create a more harmonious and whole world, and it is not simply an act of charity or goodwill.

There are many ways to show it in our daily lives. We can offer a kind word to someone who is having a tough day, help a neighbor with their groceries, or simply listen with an open heart. Every act of Chesed has the power to make a difference. We can help build a more just and loving world by choosing to be compassionate and merciful.

Tiferet - The Power of Beauty

Tiferet, often translated as "beauty," is the last of the three ethical sephirot. However, Tiferet encompasses a much broader range of meanings, including truth, balance, and harmony. In the Jewish tradition, Tiferet is often seen as the embodiment of compassion and mercy. The quality allows us to see the beauty in all things, even when they are difficult or painful. Tiferet is about finding balance amid chaos and harmony amid discord. It is a reminder that there is always hope for a better tomorrow – even in the darkest times.

The Child of Gevurah and Chesed

The sixth sephirah on the Kabbalistic Tree of Life, Tiferet, is the child of Gevurah and Chesed and embodies both of these qualities. On the one hand, Tiferet represents strength and discipline, while on the other hand, it represents compassion and mercy. This duality is what makes Tiferet such a powerful sephirah.

Tiferet teaches us that we must strike a balance between different aspects of our lives. We must be strong enough to face our challenges head-on, but we must also be compassionate enough to show mercy when needed. We hope to find true fulfillment in life by achieving this balance.

The Force of Balance

At the center of the Kabbalistic Tree of Life is the sefirah of Tiferet. This sephirah is often seen as a sign of balance because it brings together mercy and judgment, which are usually at odds with each other. Tiferet also represents the ideal human state, in which all our emotions and desires are in harmony. To achieve this balance, we must first move through a process of self-discovery, in which we come to understand our strengths and weaknesses. Only then can we learn to accept both our light and shadow sides and find the middle path that leads to wholeness. The sephirah of Tiferet reminds us that true balance comes from within, and it is only by understanding ourselves that we can hope to achieve it.

The Power of Beauty and Harmony

On a personal level, Tiferet represents our inner beauty and our ability to show that beauty to the world. When we are in touch with our own

Tiferet, we can see the beauty in others and create relationships of mutual respect and admiration. We are also able to find meaning and purpose in our lives, even in the midst of difficult challenges. The power of Tiferet lies in its ability to transform our lives from the inside out, infusing them with beauty, balance, and harmony.

The Quality of Compassion

Tiferet is often represented as a rose, as it is seen as the link between opposites such as pleasure and pain, light and dark, and love and jealousy. Tiferet occupies a central position between Binah (understanding) and Chesed (loving-kindness) in the sephirot system. This placement reflects the belief that Tiferet represents the ideal balance between these two extremes. Tiferet also encompasses all the other sefirot, which makes it a powerful symbol of compassion. After all, what could be more compassionate than accepting all aspects of reality, both the light and the dark?

Unlocking the Power of Tiferet

Tiferet is a powerful sephirah that can help us to find balance and harmony in our lives. To unlock its power, we must first learn to accept all aspects of ourselves, both the light and the shadow. Once we have done this, we can begin to see the beauty in others and find compassion for them. We can also use Tiferet's power to give our lives meaning and direction. By lining up with the sephirah of Tiferet, we can try to reach a state of balance and harmony that will make our lives more enjoyable.

One way to begin working with Tiferet is to meditate on the qualities of balance and harmony. Visualize yourself surrounded by these qualities and feel them infusing your body and mind. Allow yourself to be filled with a sense of calm and well-being. As you meditate, repeat the following mantra:

"I am in touch with my inner beauty. I am surrounded by balance and harmony. I am filled with compassion for myself and others. I am open to the possibilities of a more fulfilling life."

Another way to work with Tiferet is to focus on the quality of compassion. Visualize yourself surrounded by compassion, both for yourself and others. Allow yourself to feel the power of this quality infusing your body and mind. As you meditate, repeat the following mantra:

"I am surrounded by compassion. I am open to feeling the pain of others. I am willing to see the beauty in all things. I am committed to creating a more compassionate world."

As you work with Tiferet, remember that the goal is not to achieve perfection but to find balance and harmony in your life. Allow yourself to be imperfect, and know that this is part of the human experience. Embrace all aspects of yourself, both the light and shadow. By doing so, you will be well on your way to aligning with the sephirah of Tiferet.

The three ethical principles of Gevurah, Chesed, and Tiferet show the balance between different parts of reality. By aligning putting ourselves with these sephirot, we can strive to make our lives more balanced and harmonious. Through meditation and self-reflection, we can begin to work with these sephirot and unlock their power, and we'll create a more fulfilling life for ourselves and others. The key is to remember that the goal is not perfection but rather balance. So, embrace all aspects of yourself, both the light and the shadow. In doing so, you will be well on your way to achieving a more fulfilling life.

Chapter 6: The Sephirot III. From the Physical to the Astral

In the Kabbalistic tradition, Yetzirah is the second of the four worlds. This is the world of formation, where creative energy takes shape. The sephirot of Hod, Netzach, and Yesod are associated with this world. Hod represents rational thought and analysis, while Netzach stands for emotion and feeling. Yesod is the principle of change and transformation. It connects the other sephirot to the physical world. Yetzirah is a realm of potential and possibility where anything can be created. It is a place of imagination and creativity where we can bring our dreams and visions into reality.

The sephirot of Hod, Netzach, and Yesod are associated with this world.
Cronholm144, CC BY-SA 2.5 <https://creativecommons.org/licenses/by-sa/2.5>, via Wikimedia Commons: https://commons.wikimedia.org/wiki/File:Tree_of_life_wk_02.svg

By working with the sephirot of Hod, Netzach, and Yesod, we can tap into our creative power and create the life we want to live. In this chapter, we will explore each of these sephirot and learn how to work with them to create the life we desire. We can start to move up to the higher realm of Assiah, the world of manifestation, by using the sephirot of Yetzirah.

The Last Triad

The Tree of Life is a mysterious symbol found in many different cultures and religions. For the Kabbalists, it represents the path to enlightenment and spiritual rebirth. The Tree is divided into ten sephiroth, or spheres, each representing a different aspect of God. The last triad, Hod, Netzach, and Yesod, represents the Tikkun Olam, or "repair of the world." These three sephiroth represent the principles of right action, right thought, and right speech. Together, they help us to create a more just and harmonious world. The Trees of Life can be found in many places, from ancient Egyptian temples to modern Jewish homes. They remind us that we are all connected and that we each have a role to play in making the world a better place.

While the sephirot of Hod, Netzach, and Yesod represent the higher realms of Yetzirah, the sephirah of Malchut represents the physical plane. Malchut is the principle of manifestation; through this sephirah, we can bring our dreams and visions into reality. By working with the sephirot of Yetzirah, we can start to rise to the higher realm of Assiah, the world of manifestation.

Hod - The Splendor of God

Hod is the eighth sephirah and is associated with glory and splendor. In the Bible, Hod is often used to describe the radiance of God's presence, as in the passage from Exodus: "And Moses went into the cloud, and ascended into Mount Sinai...And the Lord descended in the cloud, and stood with him there, and proclaimed the name of the Lord."

Hod is also associated with the left-hand path, which is sometimes seen as a path of excess and indulgence. However, Hod also represents balance and harmonious relationships. In Kabbalah, Hod is often paired with Netzach, the sephirah of victory, which helps to bring power and form to Hod's visionary creativity. Together, these two sephiroth offer a complete picture of divine revelation.

Hod is connected to the element of fire and stands for the idea of doing the right thing. It is the sephirah of righteous speech, and through it, we can express our truth. When we align our words with our highest and deepest truth, we can create miracles in our lives. We can also use the power of Hod to bring our dreams and visions into reality. The sephirah of Hod is also associated with the planet Mercury and is said to rule over the sign of Gemini. Gemini is known for its dual nature, reflected in the two faces of Hod: the face of glory and the face of excess.

The path to Hod begins with the sephirah of Chesed, and it is through this sephirah that we can access our divine nature. From Chesed, we move to Geburah, and through this sephirah, we can begin to purify our thoughts and deeds. As we move through the sephiroth, we reach Tiferet, the sephirah of balance and harmony. From Tiferet, we move to Netzach, the sephirah of victory, and through this sephirah, we can begin to manifest our dreams and visions. Finally, we reach Hod, the sephirah of right action, and it is through this sephirah that we can bring our truth into the world.

Symbolism

Hod Sephirah is one of the nine sephirot of the Kabbalistic Tree of Life. It is right in the middle of the tree, below Tiferet and above Netzach. Hod corresponds to the eighth day of Creation when God said, "Let there be light." In Jewish tradition, Hod is associated with splendor, glory, and majesty. The name Hod comes from the Hebrew word meaning "splendor" or "majesty." The sephirah is also associated with the element of earth.

Hod Sephirah represents the human need for balance and harmony. It is often thought of as a place of stillness and stability amid change and flux. Hod Sephirah is a symbol for the act of receiving, which we need to do to get blessings from above. When we are receptive, we are open to change and growth. We can also think of Hod Sephirah as a place of focus where we can direct our attention and energy to manifest our desires into reality.

Unlocking Hod

Kabbalistic tradition says that the Sephirah of Hod can be opened by being kind and humble. By doing nice things for other people, we make room in our hearts and minds for all the possibilities in the universe. As we let go of our ego-driven desires, we begin to tap into a higher source of wisdom and strength.

The Sephirah of Hod is also linked to the element of water, which stands for cleanliness and movement. To open Hod, we have to be ready to let go of our attachments and let the flow of universal energy guide us. When we do things that are for the best of all, we open the door to receiving an endless supply of good things.

There are many ways to unlock the power of Hod Sephirah. One way is to meditate on the sephirah's symbol, the two-faced lion. The lion represents strength, courage, and power. As we meditate on the lion, we can visualize ourselves as powerful creators capable of manifesting our dreams into reality. We can also use the power of Hod to purify our thoughts and deeds. By aligning our actions with our highest truth, we can create miracles in our lives.

Netzach-The Victory

Netzach, which means "victory" in Hebrew, is the seventh of the 10 sephirot in the Kabbalistic Tree of Life. It is associated with the element of fire and the planet Venus. Netzach is a strong sephirah showing how good wins over evil and light over darkness. It is a symbol of hope and strength in the face of adversity.

The path to Netzach begins with the sephirah of Chesed, and it is through this sephirah that we can access our divine nature. From Chesed, we move to Geburah, where we can begin to purify our thoughts and deeds. As we move through the sephiroth, we reach Tiferet, the sephirah of balance and harmony. From Tiferet, we move to Netzach, the sephirah of victory.

It is through Netzach that we can begin to manifest our dreams and visions. This sephirah is about the power of positive thinking and the ability to overcome any obstacle. When we align our thoughts and actions with our highest truth, we can create anything we desire. The key to using Netzach's power is to believe in our ability to make things happen.

When we tap into the energy of Netzach, we align ourselves with the forces of love and justice. We open ourselves up to limitless possibilities and potential. We become warriors for truth and compassion. We can see beyond our limitations and connect with something much greater than ourselves. In short, Netzach is the sephirah of transformation. It is the spark that ignites our journey toward wholeness and enlightenment.

Symbolism

The Netzach Sephirah is often symbolized by a rose representing balance and beauty. The rose is also a symbol of the Divine Feminine, and Netzach is often seen as the Sphere of Venus. It is associated with qualities such as love, compassion, and creativity.

In the Tree of Life, Netzach is found at the bottom of the left-hand column, opposite Hod. This placement symbolizes the fact that Netzach is receptive to energy, while Hod is an active one. Together, these two Sephiroth represent the perfect balance of masculine and feminine energy. Just as a rose has both thorns and petals, so does Netzach contain light and darkness. But when these opposites are in harmony, they create something truly beautiful.

The color associated with Netzach is green, representing growth, fertility, and new beginnings. Green is the color of springtime when the world comes alive after a long winter. It is the color of hope and possibility. When we work with the energy of Netzach, we open ourselves up to new possibilities and potential. We allow ourselves to grow and expand in all directions.

In the Tarot, Netzach is represented by the suit of cups. Water, which is connected to cups, symbolizes feelings and emotions. Cups are all about relationships, both with others and with ourselves. It is through our relationships that we learn and grow. We learn about love, compassion, and forgiveness. We also learn about anger, jealousy, and pain. Ultimately, we understand who we are and what we are here to do through our relationships.

The path of Netzach is the path of the heart. It is a path of love, compassion, and forgiveness. It is a path of healing and transformation. When we walk this path, we open ourselves up to limitless possibilities. We allow ourselves to be guided by our hearts and find our way back to our true nature.

Unlocking Netzach

To unlock Netzach Sephirah, you must have completed the previous five Sephiroth. Once you have done that, you can access Netzach by meditating on the path between Binah and Chesed. When you reach Netzach, you will experience a sense of bliss and ecstasy. You may also see visions of lovely gardens or hear divine music. The key to unlocking Netzach is simply relaxing and letting yourself be open to whatever experiences come your way.

Meditation

To begin meditation, find a comfortable place to sit or lie down. Close your eyes and take a few deep breaths. Then, visualize yourself standing at the base of a great tree. This tree is the Tree of Life, and it represents your journey toward wholeness and enlightenment.

See yourself climbing the tree until you reach the fifth Sephirah, Binah. Then, continue up to the sixth Sephirah, Chesed. At Chesed, you will find a doorway leading into a beautiful garden. This is the Garden of Netzach.

Enter the garden and let yourself explore. Notice the sights, sounds, and smells around you. Listen to the birds singing and the breeze rustling through the leaves. Feel the sun on your skin and the grass beneath your feet.

As you explore the garden, you will come across a rosebush. Pluck a rose from the bush and hold it close to your heart. The rose is a symbol of Netzach Sephirah. It represents love, compassion, and beauty. As you hold the rose close to your heart, feel these qualities opening up within you.

Allow yourself to be filled with the energy of Netzach. Feel it flowing through you, around you, and within you. Listen to your heart's guidance, and let it lead you on your journey. When you are ready, begin to make your way back to the tree. Climb down the tree until you reach the ground. Then, open your eyes and return to the present moment.

Yesod - The Foundation

The Yesod Sephirah, also known as the Foundation, is the ninth and final sephirah on the Tree of Life. It is situated at the bottom of the tree, beneath the Malkuth sephirah. Yesod represents our connection to the physical world and serves as a foundation for all other sephiroth. It is associated with the Moon, which reflects the light of the Sun down to Earth.

The Yesod sephirah is also associated with memory, as it helps us to remember our past lives and experiences. Without Yesod, we would be lost in an ocean of forgetfulness. This sephirah also helps us to connect with our higher selves and access our higher consciousness. From Yesod, we can get a greater understanding of who we are and why we are here.

The Yesod Sephirah is also known as the "gateway to paradise" or the "gateway to truth." It is said to represent our connection to the divine and to be the source of all spiritual knowledge. The Yesod Sephirah is also associated with several other concepts, including balance, justice, righteousness, and integrity. As such, it is considered to be an important symbol in many different spiritual traditions.

Symbolism

The Yesod sephirah is symbolized by a cube. This is because it represents our connection to the physical world. The cube also symbolizes stability, as it has four equal sides and four equal corners. This stability helps us to remain grounded in our physical bodies and anchored in the present moment.

The color associated with Yesod is purple, the color of royalty. It represents our divine connection to the Source. Purple also symbolizes wisdom, as it is the color of the Third Eye Chakra. When we are attuned to our Third Eye Chakra, we can see beyond the physical world and access our higher consciousness.

Unlocking Yesod

Yesod can be unlocked through meditation and prayer. When we meditate on Yesod, we connect with our higher selves and access our spiritual knowledge. We can also unlock this sephirah by spending time in nature, as it helps us to remember our connection to the Earth. Furthermore, we can use crystals and stones to attune ourselves to the Yesod sephirah. Some of the most powerful crystals for this purpose include amethyst, moonstone, and labradorite.

When we work with the Yesod sephirah, we access our higher consciousness and connect with our spiritual truth. We also remember our past lives and experiences, which helps us to understand our present situation. We can better understand who we are and why we are here from Yesod.

Malchut - The Kingdom

The Malchut sephirah, also known as the Kingdom, is the tenth and final sephirah on the Tree of Life. It is found at the bottom of the tree, beneath the Yesod sephirah. Malchut represents our connection to the physical world and serves as a foundation for all other sephiroth. It is associated with the element of Earth, which is the material foundation of our lives. The Malchut sephirah is also associated with the planet Saturn, which is the planet of structure and stability.

As the final sephirah on the Tree of Life, Malchut represents our journey back to the Source. It is the sephirah of return, and it reminds us that all things must come to an end. From Malchut, we learn about death and rebirth and the cyclical nature of life. We can also gain a greater understanding of our place in the universe.

Symbolism

A crown symbolizes the Malchut sephirah. This is because it represents our connection to the physical world. The crown also symbolizes our journey back to the Source, reminding us that we are all royalty in the eyes of the Divine. Malchut's color is green, representing growth, abundance, and fertility. Green is also the color of the Heart Chakra, which is associated with love and compassion.

Unlocking Malchut

In the Kabbalah, Malchut is the sephirah that represents the realm of earthly experience. Through our connection to Malchut, we interact with the physical world and manifest our desires. When we are cut off from Malchut, we become disconnected from our true purpose and lose sight of what is important. The good news is that it is possible to unlock Malchut and reconnect with our source of power. By meditating on the sephirah and performing certain rituals, we can open the door to a richer, more fulfilling existence and begin to experience the world in a whole new way.

When we meditate on Malchut, we connect with our higher selves and access our spiritual knowledge. Another way to unlock this sephirah is by spending time in nature, as it reminds us of our connection to the Earth. Not only can we use crystals and stones to attune ourselves to the Malchut sephirah, but doing so can also help improve our connection with the divine. Some of the most powerful crystals for this purpose include emerald, jade, and green tourmaline.

How Malchut Represents the Physical Plane

Kabbalah teaches that there are four planes of existence: the physical, emotional, mental, and spiritual. Each plane is represented by one of the sephirot or divine attributes. The physical plane is represented by

Malchut, which means "kingdom." This is because the physical plane is the kingdom of matter, where things are solid and tangible. Mastering the physical plane requires learning how to control and use the material world in a way that benefits all. When we live in harmony with the physical plane, we can create a peaceful and just world that provides everything we need.

How Malchut Relates to the Other Sephirot

Malchut is often viewed as the lowest of the sephirot, but this is only because it is the last sephirah in the descending order. In reality, Malchut is just as important as any of the other sephirot. It represents the final stage of manifestation, where the spiritual energy of the other sephirot is condensed into physical form. Without Malchut, there would be no way to experience the divine on a physical level.

Malchut also is a bridge between the spiritual and physical worlds. Through Malchut, we can interact with the divine realm and receive guidance from Above. Finally, Malchut also represents our unique individuality. Each of us has a unique role to play in the world; through Malchut, we can express our uniqueness. Without Malchut, we would be indistinguishable from one another. As you can see, Malchut is a vital part of the cosmic order and plays an essential role in our lives.

The sephirot you have just covered are Hod, Netzach, and Yesod (from the Kabbalistic realm of Yetzirah) as well as Malchut (from Assiah, the physical realm). These four sephirot represent the last stage of manifestation, where the spiritual energy of the other sephirot is condensed into physical form. Each sephirah plays a vital role in our lives and helps us interact more deeply with the world.

Chapter 7: The Archangels of the Tree of Life

In Judaism, angels are regarded as the intermediaries between God and humanity. They are believed to play an important role in guiding and protecting people on their spiritual journeys. In Kabbalah, they are seen as reflections of different aspects of God and are thought to be messengers from the divine realm who bring mystical knowledge and insights. Angels are also sometimes invoked in Jewish prayers and rituals. For example, people often say that reading the Torah is like getting advice from an angel. In general, angels are considered powerful spiritual beings who can help us connect with the Divine.

The
**Qabalistic
Tree of Life**
(With Enochian Correspondences)

LEGEND

Each of the sephirot on the Tree of Life is represented by an archangel.
*VendettaXIII, CC BY-SA 4.0 <https://creativecommons.org/licenses/by-sa/4.0>, via Wikimedia
Commons: https://commons.wikimedia.org/wiki/File:Qabbalah-tree-of-life.jpg*

Each of the sephirot on the Tree of Life is represented by an archangel. In this chapter, we will illustrate which angel belongs to which sphere. Then, we will go through each sephirah again, this time focusing only on the archangel that represents it. We will explain why that angelic being is connected to that sephirah, describe the characteristics of that archangel, their role as well as how they can help the reader, and lastly, include a short prayer dedicated to that archangel.

The Archangels of the Tree of Life

The Tree of Life, often seen as a connection between heaven and earth, represents the path we take through life. The archangels are powerful celestial beings who are said to watch over us as we travel along this path. There are ten archangels, each of whom is associated with one of the 10 sephirot on the Tree of Life. These include Metatron (Kether), Raziel (Chokmah), Tzaphkiel (Binah), Tzadkiel (Chesed), Kamael (Geburah), Raphael (Tipheret), Haneil (Netzach), Michael (Hod), Gabriel (Yesod), and Sandalphon (Malkuth).

The Archangel of Kether: Metatron

Kether, the highest sphere of the Tree of Life, is home to the Archangel Metatron. As the "Prince of Countenance," he is the angel who stands before the face of God. Metatron is said to be responsible for recording and maintaining all of God's thoughts and plans. He is also the angel who transmits God's will to humanity. In Jewish tradition, Metatron is sometimes called "the voice of God." In reality, he is the one who brings God and people together. Metatron is a powerful and influential figure in both Jewish and Christian mysticism. His name means "he who occupies the throne next to the Divine Throne." He is a very near and special Angel to God Himself.

Characteristics

Metatron is a powerful and wise being who serves as a guide and protector for humanity. Metatron is usually shown as a young man with wings holding a sword or a staff. He is also said to be very tall, with a shining countenance. Some traditions identify Metatron as the Angel of the Covenant or the Scribe of God. In Jewish tradition, he is known as the man who led Abraham out of Ur and into Canaan. In the New Testament, he is mentioned as the angel who appeared to Moses in the burning bush. Metatron is a powerful and wise being and a strong ally for those who want help and protection.

Role

Archangel Metatron is the ruler of all the angels and the protector of all of God's secrets. He is also the scribe of God because it is said that he has recorded everything that has ever been written. Archangel Metatron is a powerful being often called upon to help us in our time of need. He is said to be able to manifest anything that we need, and he can also help us understand life's mysteries. When we call upon Archangel Metatron, we ask for his help to guide us on our path.

A Prayer to Metatron

Dear Archangel Metatron,

Thank you for your guidance and protection. You are a powerful being who knows all of God's secrets. Help us understand life's mysteries and manifest what we need. We call upon you in our time of need and ask that you help us find our way. Thank you for your wisdom and your strength.

Amen.

The Archangel of Chokmah: Raziel

Raziel is the archangel of wisdom and knowledge. Raziel is a powerful being who can help us to understand the hidden knowledge of the universe. He is said to be the keeper of all of God's secrets and is known as the "Angel of Mysteries." Raziel is often depicted as a man with wings, holding a book or scroll in his hand. In Jewish tradition, Raziel is known as the "Great Angel" or the "Prince of Angels." He is also said to be the angel who taught Adam and Eve about the secrets of life.

Characteristics

Raziel is the Archangel of Chokmah, the divine wisdom of God. He is often depicted as a powerful and radiant being shrouded in light. Raziel is known for his great wisdom and knowledge and is said to be a master of all spiritual mysteries. He is also a guide and teacher, helping souls to remember their true nature and purpose. Raziel is a fierce protector of the innocent and a powerful force for good. He is often called upon in times of trouble or crisis, and his presence can bring hope and comfort. He is a miraculous being, and his guidance can help us navigate life's challenges with grace and ease.

Role

Raziel represents wisdom and understanding. In Jewish tradition, Raziel is known as the angel of secrets and mysteries. Raziel is also associated with the element of water. This is fitting, as water is often seen as a symbol of knowledge and understanding. In many traditions, Raziel is also known as the angel of judgment. This is because he is said to preside over the weighing of souls in the afterlife. As the Archangel of Chokmah, Raziel represents all that is wise and intelligent in the universe. He is a powerful ally for those seeking to understand existence's secrets.

Prayer to Raziel

Dear Archangel Raziel,

Thank you for your wisdom and guidance. You are the keeper of all of God's secrets and master of all spiritual mysteries. Help us to remember our true nature and purpose, and lead us on our path with grace and ease. We call upon you in times of trouble or crisis and know that your presence will bring us comfort and hope. Thank you for your compassion and your wisdom.

Amen.

The Archangel of Binah: Tzaphkiel

Tzaphkiel is the archangel of Binah, the third Sefira. Binah is associated with understanding, insight, and Wisdom, and Tzaphkiel is often invoked when seeking to gain knowledge or clarity. He is also known as the "Angel of Silence" because he infuses our hearts with Divine understanding. When we turn to Tzaphkiel for guidance, we open ourselves up to greater insight and understanding. In doing so, we align ourselves more closely with the Divine Will.

Characteristics

Binah is understanding, and Tzaphkiel helps us to understand ourselves and the world around us. He is also the angel of "divine will" and can help us to align our own will with that of the Divine. Tzaphkiel has a calm and gentle energy and is a great angel to call upon when we need clarity and guidance. He can also help us to let go of negative patterns and behaviors that no longer serve us. Call on Tzaphkiel, the kind archangel of Binah, if you want to understand your life or get help with it.

Role

Tzaphkiel helps us to see both the eternal and temporal aspects of reality and to understand their relationships to one another. Tzaphkiel also helps us reach the higher levels of consciousness we need to grow spiritually. One of the most crucial things that Tzaphkiel teaches us is that everything is connected. Everything that exists in the universe is interrelated, and it is only through understanding these relationships that we can achieve true wisdom. Tzaphkiel also reminds us that love is the most powerful force in the universe. When we open our hearts to love, we can tap into a vast reservoir of power and wisdom. By following Tzaphkiel's teachings, we can learn to live in harmony with all of creation.

Prayer to Tzaphkiel

Dear Archangel Tzaphkiel,

Thank you for your guidance and wisdom. You are the angel of understanding and help us see the interconnectedness of all things. You teach us that everything is connected and that love is the most powerful force in the universe. Help us to align our will with the Divine Will, and lead us on our path with grace and ease.

Amen.

The Archangel of Chesed: Tzadkiel

Archangel Tzadkiel is the Angel of Chesed or Loving-Kindness. He is called the "Prince of Mercy," and people often ask for his help when they need to forgive someone. Tzadkiel also presides over Wednesday, the day of Mercury. In Jewish tradition, Tzadkiel is also known as "Sachiel," and he is associated with the Sefirah of Netzach. In Kabbalah, Tzadkiel is seen as a powerful mediator between the Divine Will and human actions. He is said to bring our prayers before the Throne of Grace and is known for his ability to infuse our lives with Chesed. Archangel Tzadkiel is a potent force for good in the world, and he can be called upon for help in times of need.

Characteristics

The Archangel of Chesed, Tzadkiel, is known for his compassion and mercy. He is often invoked in times of trouble or hardship, as he is said to bring comfort and peace. Tzadkiel is also known for his ability to help us forgive ourselves and others and let go of emotions like anger, resentment, and bitterness. In Jewish tradition, Tzadkiel is associated with the sefirah of Chesed, which represents loving-kindness and compassion. Chesed is the divine quality that allows us to give and receive love unconditionally. It is the force that binds us together as a community and helps us to nurture and care for one another. Tzadkiel reminds us that we are all connected and that we each have the capacity for great love and compassion.

Role

In Jewish thought, Chesed is one of the highest virtues. It encompasses everything from compassion and mercy to forgiveness and generosity. Tzadkiel's role is to help us cultivate Chesed in our own lives. When we act with Chesed, we fulfill God's will and make the world better. As well as being the angel of Chesed, Tzadkiel is also associated with tzedakah or charity. He reminds us that we must help those less fortunate than ourselves. By giving our time, energy, and resources, we can make a real difference in the lives of others. Following Tzadkiel's example, we can learn to be more compassionate and caring.

Prayer to Tzadkiel

Dear Archangel Tzadkiel,

Thank you for your mercy and compassion. You are the angel of Chesed, and you remind us that we are all connected. You teach us the importance of giving and receiving love unconditionally. Help us to open our hearts to Chesed, and lead us on our path with grace and ease.

Amen.

The Archangel of Geburah: Kamael

Kamael is the Archangel of Geburah, one of the seven primary Archangels who rule over the Seven Heavens. He is known as the "Sovereign of Justice" and is said to dispense divine retribution. Kamael is also associated with strength, courage, and fortitude. He is often illustrated as carrying a sword or wielding a lightning bolt. Some believe that Kamael fell from grace after refusing to bow down to humans. As a result, he was cast out of Heaven and became the ruler of Hell. However, other stories say that Kamael remains in Heaven, protecting those who have been wronged. No matter his current whereabouts, Kamael is a powerful force for good and evil. He is a reminder that even the mightiest can fall but that redemption is always possible.

Characteristics

Kamael is the Archangel of Geburah, a powerful warrior and an avenging angel; he is known for his justice and righteousness. Kamael is also known as the "Slayer of Kings" and the "Destroyer of Worlds." He is a fierce opponent of evil and injustice, and he will not hesitate to fight against those who threaten the peace and harmony of the Universe. Kamael is a powerful ally in the fight against evil, and he will stand with those who are righteous and just. He is a force for good in the world and will help those who seek to do right. Kamael is a friend to all who are good and an enemy to all who are evil. He is the Archangel of Geburah and will always fight for what is right.

Role

According to angelic lore, the archangel Kamael is the ruler of the fifth heaven and one of the Seven Archangels who stand before the throne of God. As the Archangel of Geburah, Kamael represents strength, power, and judgment. In Jewish tradition, Kamael is often equated with Samael, the Angel of Death. However, in other belief systems, Kamael is considered a force for good, helping protect humanity from evil forces. Whether seen as a bringer of death or a defender of life, the Archangel Kamael is an important figure in many spiritual traditions.

Prayer to Kamael

Dear Archangel Kamael,

Thank you for your strength and courage. You are the Archangel of Geburah, and you dispense divine justice. You are a powerful ally in the fight against evil and will always fight for what is right. Help us to stand against injustice and evil, and lead us to a life of peace and harmony.

Amen.

The Archangel of Tiphareth: Raphael

Raphael is the Archangel of Tiphareth, the fifth Sephirah on the Tree of Life. He is known as the "healing angel" and is associated with green and pink colors. Raphael is often shown with a staff or wand in his hand, and a six-winged seraph is his symbol. Raphael's job as the Archangel of

Tiphareth is to help souls reach their highest potential. He helps us to tap into our creativity and bliss and brings healing energy into our lives. When we call upon Raphael, we open ourselves up to receive his guidance and support. In doing so, we can create more harmonious lives for ourselves and those around us.

Characteristics

Raphael is one of the most important archangels in Judaism, Christianity, and Islam. He is known as the "angel of healing" or the "angel of hope." Raphael is often shown holding a staff or a scroll. He is also associated with the sun and with the color green. In the Book of Tobit, Raphael disguised himself as a man and helped Tobias to find a wife and cure his father's blindness. In the Bible, Raphael is one of the seven archangels standing before God's throne. In Islam, Raphael is known as Israfil and is responsible for blowing the trumpet on Judgment Day. Raphael is a powerful and benevolent angel who can help us in times of need.

Role

Raphael is associated with the element of air; his name means "healing" or "medicine" in Hebrew. Raphael is often depicted holding a staff or wand, which represents his power to heal, and he is also known as the Angel of Deliverance. He is a powerful ally for anyone seeking physical and emotional healing and can also help protect against disease. Raphael is also known for bringing peace and harmony, and people often call on him when there is trouble. Whether you are seeking healing for yourself or someone else, calling on Raphael can help to bring about positive change.

Prayer to Raphael

Dear Archangel Raphael,

Thank you for your healing energy. You are the Angel of Deliverance and bring hope and healing into our lives. You are associated with the element of air and help us breathe life into our dreams. You guide us toward our highest potential and help us create more harmonious lives.

Amen.

The Archangel of Netzach: Haniel

Haniel is the angel of beauty, inspiration, and grace. Her name means "glory of God," and she is usually shown with a bouquet or a crystal orb in her hands. As the Archangel of Netzach, Haniel governs the seventh chakra, which is associated with the colors pink and green. Haniel helps us to connect with our higher selves and tap into our creative potential. She is a powerful ally in times of Transition when we seek guidance on our life path. Haniel's energy is feminine and receptive, and she reminds us that sometimes the best thing to do is just to let our dreams and desires come true when they are ready. When we call on Haniel, we open ourselves up to a world of possibility.

Characteristics

Haniel is the Archangel of Netzach, the seventh Sephira on the Tree of Life. Netzach represents the spiritual victory over the material, and Haniel helps us achieve this victory. Haniel is often associated with the planet Venus; her name means "glory" or "grace." She brings us beauty, sweetness, and love. Haniel also helps us to connect with our higher selves and our Angels. We can call on Haniel to help us achieve our goals and manifest our desires. Haniel's energy is feminine and receptive, and we can call on Haniel to help us balance our masculine and feminine energies. She is a powerful ally in our spiritual journey.

Role

The Archangel of Netzach is Haniel. Netzach is the seventh sephira on the Tree of Life. It is situated at the bottom right of the tree and is represented by the planet Venus. The name Netzach means "victory" or "eternity." It is also associated with the concepts of love, beauty, and nature. As the Archangel of Netzach, Haniel is responsible for helping us to connect with these qualities. She helps us to see the beauty in all things and appreciate the natural world around us. Haniel also inspires us to pursue our dreams and never give up. No matter what challenges we face, Haniel reminds us that we have the inner strength to overcome them and achieve our goals.

Prayer to Haniel

Dear Archangel Haniel,

Thank you for your guidance and inspiration. You are the Angel of Netzach, and you help us to see the beauty in all things. You are associated with the planet Venus, and you bring us love, beauty, and harmony. Thank you for your help in bringing more balance into our lives.

Amen.

The Archangel of Hod: Michael

The Archangel of Hod, Michael, is known for his strength and power. He is one of the most popular angels in Catholicism and Christianity and is often depicted as a powerful warrior. In the Bible, Michael is described as the leader of God's army and said to have defeated Satan in a battle in heaven. In addition to his role as a protector, Michael is also known as the Angel of Healing. He is said to bring comfort to those who are suffering and provide them with strength in times of need. For Christians, Michael is a powerful symbol of hope and protection, and his image can be found in churches around the world.

Characteristics

Archangel Michael is the Archangel of Hod, which means "Glory." He is associated with protection, healing, and salvation. As the Archangel of Hod, Michael is responsible for helping us to manifest our highest potential. He is also known as the Prince of Angels and is considered the leader of the archangels. Archangel Michael is said to be the most powerful of all the archangels. He is often depicted holding a sword or wearing armor. He is also associated with the color blue. Archangel Michael can help you to connect with your higher self, heal old wounds, and protect yourself from negative energy. If you are seeking guidance or protection, Archangel Michael can help you to find your way.

Role

Archangel Michael is the archangel of protection, strength, and courage. He is known as the defender of the faith and the patron saint of policemen and soldiers. Archangel Michael is also known as the Prince of Angels and the leader of God's army. He is often depicted holding a sword or wearing armor. Archangel Michael is a powerful intercessor and protector. He is invoked for protection from danger, disease, and violence. Archangel Michael also helps us to let go of fear, worry, and doubt. He fills us with strength, courage, and peace when we call on him.

Prayer to Archangel Michael

Dear Archangel Michael,

Thank you for your protection and guidance. You are the Archangel of Hod, and you help us to manifest our highest potential. You are the leader of the archangels and the patron saint of policemen and soldiers. Thank you for filling us with strength, courage, and peace when we call on you.

Amen.

The Archangel of Yesod: Gabriel

Of all the archangels, Gabriel is perhaps the best known. He is the angel of revelation and delivered the news of Jesus' birth to the Virgin Mary. In addition, Gabriel is also associated with the Moon card in tarot readings. This card represents new beginnings, emotional depths, and hidden truths. Gabriel can be seen as a symbol of divine guidance and spiritual inspiration. So whatever your goal or challenge may be, remember that you can always call on Gabriel to help achieve it.

Characteristics

The Archangel of Yesod is Gabriel. He stands at the gate of Eden, and his task is to keep the way of the Tree of Life clear for humanity. He is also responsible for guiding souls to their proper place in the afterlife. Gabriel is a powerful angel; his strength lies in his ability to help others. He is a guardian angel, and he will protect those who are under his care. He is also a teacher and will help those who want to learn about the Tree of Life. Gabriel is a kind and compassionate angel who will always be there to help those who need it.

Prayer to Archangel Gabriel

Dear Archangel Gabriel,

Thank you for your guidance and protection. You are the Archangel of Yesod, and you are responsible for keeping the way of the Tree of Life clear for humanity. You are a guardian angel, and you will protect those who are under your care. You are also a teacher and will help those who want to learn about the Tree of Life.

Amen.

The Archangel of Malkuth: Sandalphon

Sandalphon is the Archangel of Malkuth, the tenth and final sephira on the Tree of Life. He is called the "messenger of God" and is often shown holding a scroll or a trumpet. Sandalphon is in charge of directing our prayers to Heaven and conveying Divine messages. He is also a protector of Earth and its creatures. In many ways, Sandalphon is the perfect guardian angel for our world. He is committed to assisting us in finding a happy medium between them. If we ever feel lost or disconnected from the Divine, we can call on Sandalphon for guidance. He will help us find our way back home.

Characteristics

Sandalphon is known as the "Heavenly Scribe," and he is responsible for communicating our prayers to God. He is also known as the "Angel of Music" because he helps us connect with the divine melodies of the universe. Sandalphon is closely connected to Mother Earth; he helps us be grounded and anchor our energy in the physical world. He also helps us connect with our ancestors and the wisdom of our elders. Sandalphon is a powerful Archangel who can help us to manifest our desires and bring our prayers to fruition.

Prayer to Archangel Sandalphon

Dear Archangel Sandalphon,

Thank you for your guidance and protection. You are the Archangel of Malkuth and are responsible for guiding our prayers to Heaven. You are also a protector of the Earth and its creatures. In many ways, you are the perfect guardian angel for our world. You understand both the material and spiritual realms and are dedicated to helping us find a balance between them.

Amen.

The Archangels play an important role in Judaism mysticism and Kabbalah. They are responsible for guiding our prayers up to Heaven, delivering messages from the Divine, and protecting us from harm. They are also powerful symbols of divine guidance and spiritual inspiration. So whatever your goal or challenge may be, remember that you can always call on the Archangels to help achieve it.

Chapter 8: The Twenty-Two Paths and Major Arcana

For several reasons, Hebrew is considered to be a divine or mystical language. The language is unique in that it is alphabetical and also pictographic. In other words, each letter of the Hebrew alphabet is not only a letter but *also a word and a concept.* For example, the first letter of the Hebrew alphabet, Aleph, is also the word for "ox." This connection between the written and pictorial representations of words gives Hebrew a depth of meaning that other languages lack.

Each path has an association with a Major Arcana card.

This chapter will explore the connection between the Hebrew alphabet, the 22 paths on the Tree of Life, and the 22 Major Arcana cards in tarot. We will go through each path and explain its symbolism and association with its corresponding Major Arcana card.

The Hebrew Alphabet and the Tree of Life

The Hebrew Alphabet is a mystical tool that has been used for centuries to unlock the Universe's secrets. Tradition says that each letter of the alphabet represents a different level of reality and that by meditating on the letters, one can learn about the hidden parts of life. The Tree of Life is a central symbol in Hebrew mysticism, and it is said that the letters of the alphabet are like the branches of the tree, with each one leading to a different level of understanding.

In recent years, scientists have begun exploring the potential links between the Hebrew Alphabet and quantum physics, and many believe that this ancient system is the key to unlocking the mysteries of our Universe. Whether you are a seeker of knowledge or just curious about the mysteries of life, the Hebrew Alphabet is sure to offer you new insights and understanding.

The 22 Paths and the Major Arcana

Like many of the world's great religions, the tree of life is a symbol of rebirth and growth. The tree of life has 22 paths, representing the tarot's major arcana. Each path leads to a different destination, and each destination has its meaning. For example, the first path leads to the gates of paradise, while the last path leads to the underworld. In between, some paths represent love, death, and redemption. The Tree of Life is a beautiful symbol of the journey we all take. It is a reminder that there is always hope for growth and change. Whether at the beginning or the end of our journey, we can always find new paths to explore.

1. The Path of Aleph and the Fool

The Path of Aleph is the first path on the Tree of Life, representing new beginnings. This path connects the sephirot of Kether and Chokmah, and its symbolic meaning is primal energy. The Fool is often associated with this path, as this card is about taking risks and embracing the unknown. The Fool can also represent change and transformation.

2. The Path of Beth and the Magician

The second path on the Tree of Life is the Path of Beth, which represents knowledge and understanding. It connects the sephirot of Kether and Binah, and its symbolic meaning is attention. This path is

---

often linked to The Magician because this card is about using your knowledge and skills to make your own reality. The Magician is also a symbol of resourcefulness and creativity.

3. The Path of Gimel and the High Priestess

The third path on the Tree of Life is the Path of Gimel, which represents intuition and wisdom. The Path of Gimel connects the sephirot of Kether and Tiphereth and is symbolic of receptivity. The High Priestess is often associated with this path, as she symbolizes intuition and mystery. The High Priestess also reminds us that we all have access to hidden knowledge.

4. The Path of Daleth and the Empress

The fourth path on the Tree of Life is the Path of Daleth, which represents fertility and creation. The Path of Daleth connects the sephirot of Chokmah and Binah and is associated with nourishment. Since the Empress is a symbol of motherhood and femininity, it is often linked to this path. The Empress also reminds us that we are all connected to the natural world.

5. The Path of Heh and the Emperor

The Path of Heh, representing authority and structure, is the fifth path on the Tree of Life. The Path of Heh connects the sephirot of Chokmah and Tiphereth and is associated with reasoning. The Emperor is often linked to this path, as it is a symbol of strength and stability. The Emperor also reminds us that we all have the power to create our own rules and boundaries.

6. The Path of Vav and the Hierophant

The Path of Vav is the sixth path on the Tree of Life, representing balance and harmony. The Path of Vav connects the sephirot of Chokmah and Chesed and is associated with connections. The Hierophant is often linked to this path, as it symbolizes understanding and tradition. The Hierophant also reminds us that we are all part of a larger community.

7. The Path of Zain and the Lovers

The seventh path on the Tree of Life is the Path of Zain, which represents relationships and choices. The Path of Zain connects the sephirot of Binah and Tiphereth and is associated with discernment. The Lovers card is often linked to this path, as it is about making decisions based on our hearts. The Lovers is also a reminder that we are all connected.

8. The Path of Cheth and the Chariot

The eighth path on the Tree of Life is the Path of Cheth, which represents victory and success. The Path of Cheth connects the sephirot of Binah and Geburah and is associated with a field. The Chariot is often linked to this path, as it is a symbol of triumph. The Chariot is also a reminder that we all have the power to achieve our goals.

9. The Path of Teth and the Strength

The Path of Teth is the ninth path on the Tree of Life, representing courage and strength. The Path of Teth links the sephirot of Geburah to that of Tiphereth, and it is related to willpower. Strength is often linked to this path, as it is a card about using our inner strength to overcome obstacles. Strength is also a reminder that we are all capable of overcoming challenges.

10. The Path of Yod and the Hermit

The Path of Yod is the tenth path on the Tree of Life, which is all about introspection and contemplation. The Path of Yod connects the sephirot of Chesed and Tipareth and is associated with deed and work. The Hermit is often linked to this path, as it is a symbol of solitude and reflection. The Hermit also reminds us that we all need time to connect with our higher selves.

11. The Path of Kaph and the Wheel of Fortune

The Path of Kaph is the eleventh path on the Tree of Life, representing change and luck. The Path of Kaph connects the sephirot of Chesed and Netzach, and it is associated with a wheel. The Wheel of Fortune is often linked to this path, symbolizing life's ups and downs. The Wheel of Fortune is also a reminder that we all experience highs and lows, but we always have the power to change our circumstances.

12. The Path of Lamed and the Justice

The twelfth path on the Tree of Life is the Path of Lamed, which represents balance and fairness. The Path of Lamed is associated with balance and connects the sephirot of Geburah and Chesed. Justice is often linked to this path, as it is a symbol of making sure that we are living our lives in a way that is fair to ourselves and others. Justice also reminds us that we all have the power to create our destiny.

13. The Path of Mem and the Hanged Man

The thirteenth path on the Tree of Life is the Path of Mem, which represents sacrifice and surrender. The Path of Mem connects the sephirot of Geburah and Hod, and it is associated with water. The Hanged Man is often linked to this path, as it symbolizes letting go and being open to change. The Hanged Man is also a reminder that we all have the power to let go of our past and start fresh.

14. The Path of Nun and Death

The fourteenth path on the Tree of Life is the Path of Nun, which represents transformation and rebirth. The Path of Nun connects the sephirot of Tiphareth and Netzach, and it is associated with a fish. Death is often linked to this path, as it is a symbol of transformation and new beginnings. Death is a lesson that we all can let go of our past selves and begin anew.

15. The Path of Samech and Temperance

The fifteenth path on the Tree of Life is the Path of Samech, which represents moderation and balance. The Path of Samech connects the sephirot of Tiphareth and Yesod and is associated with an hourglass. Temperance is often linked to this path, as it symbolizes finding balance in our lives. Temperance also reminds us that we all have the power to create our destiny.

16. The Path of Ayin and the Devil

The sixteenth path on the Tree of Life is the Path of Ayin, which represents temptation and materialism. The Path of Ayin connects the sephirot of Tiphareth and Hod, and it is associated with a snake. The Devil is often linked to this path, as it is a symbol of our darker side. The Devil is also a reminder that we all have the power to resist temptation and stay on the path of righteousness.

17. The Path of Peh and the Tower

The Path of Peh is the seventeenth path on the Tree of Life, representing destruction and chaos. The Path of Peh connects the sephirot of Netzach and Hod, and it is associated with a lightning bolt. The Tower is often linked to this path, as it symbolizes our need to face our fears head-on. The Tower is also a reminder that we all have the power to overcome our fears and rise above them.

18. The Path of Tzaddi and the Star

The eighteenth path on the Tree of Life is the Path of Tzaddi, which represents hope and guidance. The Path of Tzaddi connects the sephirot of Netzach and Yesod, and it is associated with an anchor. The Star is often linked to this path, as it is a symbol of hope and guidance. The Star is also a reminder that we all have the power to find our way in life, no matter how lost we feel.

19. The Path of Qoph and the Moon

The nineteenth path on the Tree of Life is the Path of Qoph, representing illusion and deception. The Path of Qoph connects the sephirot of Netzach and Malkuth and is associated with hiding. The Moon is often linked to this path, symbolizing our ability to see through the illusions in life. The Moon is also a reminder that we all have the power to find our way in life, no matter how dark or chaotic it may seem.

20. The Path of Resh and the Sun

The eighteenth path on the Tree of Life is the Path of Resh, which represents enlightenment and happiness. The Path of Resh connects the sephirot of Hod and Yesod, and it is associated with redemption. The Sun is often linked to this path, as it symbolizes our ability to find joy amid the darkness. The Sun is also a reminder that we all have the power to find our inner light and let it shine forth.

21. The Path of Shin and Judgment

The nineteenth path on the Tree of Life is the Path of Shin, which represents rebirth and new beginnings. The Path of Shin connects the sephirot of Hod and Malkuth, and it is associated with a fire. Judgment is often linked to this path, as it symbolizes our ability to start anew – and it also reminds us that we all have the power to create our destiny.

22. The Path of Taw and the World

The twentieth path on the Tree of Life is the Path of Taw, which represents completion and fulfillment. The Path of Taw connects the sephirot of Malkuth and Yesod and is associated with truth. The World is often linked to this path, as it symbolizes our ability to find wholeness and completion. The World is also a reminder that we all have the power to create our reality.

Kabbalistic Tarot Reading: Reversed Cards

If you pull a reversed tarot card, it means that the energy of that card is currently blocked in your life. This can be interpreted in several ways, depending on which card you pull. For example, if you pull The Tower reversed, it could mean that you are currently facing some fears or challenges head-on. Alternatively, it could also mean that you are in the process of overcoming your fears. If you pull The Star reversed, it could mean that you are currently feeling lost or directionless. Alternatively, it could also mean that you are in the process of finding your way.

The reversed cards in your reading suggest you are not facing up to some of the challenges in your life. You may be feeling overwhelmed or stuck, and you may be avoiding difficult situations. The reversed cards also suggest that you are not seeing the whole picture and not taking all the available options into account. You may need to take a step back and reassess your situation. Look at things from a different perspective, and consider all of the possible outcomes. Be willing to make changes and take risks. The reversed cards indicate the potential for growth and transformation if you are willing to face your fears and take action.

The Tree of Life comprises 10 sephirot, which are connected by 22 paths. These paths are associated with the 22 letters of the Hebrew alphabet. The Tree of Life symbolizes our ability to find balance and harmony in our lives. The sephirot represent different aspects of our being, and the paths represent the journey we take to find wholeness. Each path has its own symbolism and meaning, which can be used to interpret the tarot. Tarot is a tool that can be used to help us understand the journey that we are on. This chapter has provided a brief overview of the Tree of Life and its connection to the tarot.

Chapter 9: The Tree of Life and Minor Arcana

In the previous chapter, we explored the Tree of Life and the Major Arcana cards associated with each of the sephirot. In this chapter, we will continue our exploration of the Tree of Life by looking at the Minor Arcana cards and their connections to the four worlds, the four elements, and the four suites. We will also discover how the sephirot correspond to the numerical values of the Minor Arcana cards. Finally, we will see how this kabbalistic method can be used for readings.

Assiah	Yetzirah	Beri'ah	Atziluth
World of Manifestation Body Faculty of Sensation	World of Formation Psyche Faculty of Thinking	World of Creation Spirit Faculty of Feeling	World of Emanation Divine Faculty of Intuition
ה	ו	ה	י
HE	VAU	HE	YOD
Pentacles	*Swords*	*Cups*	*Wands*
Earth	Air	Water	Fire

The Minor Arcana is a deck of tarot cards that represent the everyday challenges we face in life.

Tree of Life in Conjunction with Minor Arcana

The Tree of Life represents the interconnectedness of all life and how necessary balance is. The tree branches represent life's journey, while the leaves represent different parts of life. The roots represent our connection to the past, and the trunk represents our present self. The Tree of Life is also often used to symbolize the four stages of life: birth, growth, death, and rebirth.

The Minor Arcana is a deck of tarot cards that represent the everyday challenges we face in life. The Swords suit shows our thoughts and mental challenges, and the Wands suit shows our actions and physical challenges. The suit of Cups represents our emotional challenges, while the suit of Pentacles represents our material and financial challenges. Each one contains fourteen cards, divided into four groups: Ace through Ten, Page, Knight, and Queen. These groups represent the different stages of life: birth (Ace), growth (Page), death (Knight), and rebirth (Queen).

When we look at the Tree of Life and Minor Arcana together, we can see that they both symbolize life's journey. The Tree of Life shows us that every stage of life is connected, and we must maintain a balance between all areas of our existence. The Minor Arcana reminds us that challenges are a natural part of life and that we must face them head-on to grow and learn. Together, these symbols can help us navigate life's ups and downs with wisdom and grace.

The Four Worlds

The Tree of Life is divided into four worlds: Assiah, Yetzirah, Briah, and Atziluth. Each of these worlds is associated with a different element. Assiah is the world of manifestation, and its element is Earth. Yetzirah is the world of formation and is associated with the element of air. Briah is the world of creation, fire is its element, and Atziluth is the world of emanation. It is associated with the element of water.

Each of the four worlds is also associated with a different suite of Minor Arcana cards. Assiah is linked to the suit of Pentacles, Yetzirah to the suit of Swords, Briah to the suit of Wands, and Atziluth to the suit of Cups.

The Four Elements

The Tree of Life is also divided into four elements: fire, water, air, and earth. The four suits of the Minor Arcana, Wands (fire), Cups (water),

Swords (air), and Pentacles (earth), represent these four elements. Each element is associated with a different stage of life: fire is associated with birth, water is associated with growth, the air is associated with death, and earth is associated with rebirth.

The Four Suites

The Minor Arcana is divided into four suites: Swords, Wands, Cups, and Pentacles. Each of these suites is connected to a different world: the Swords are connected to Assiah, the Wands to Yetzirah, the Cups to Briah, and the Pentacles to Atziluth.

The Sephirot and the Numerical Correspondences of the Minor Arcana

In the Kabbalistic tradition, the Sephirot are 10 emanations of the Divine that represent different aspects of God's nature. Each Sephirah has its own symbol and numerical correspondence, and these correspondences can be used to unlock the hidden meanings of the Minor Arcana in a Tarot reading. The first Sephirah, Kether, is linked with the number one and represents the Divine will or purpose. The second Sephirah, Chokmah, is associated with the number two and represents wisdom or understanding.

The third Sephirah, Binah, is coupled with the number three, representing knowledge or understanding. The fourth Sephirah, Chesed, is connected with the number four, representing mercy or compassion, while the fifth Sephirah, Geburah, is associated with the number five and represents strength or power.

The sixth Sephirah, Tiphareth, is associated with the number six and represents beauty or balance. Netzach, the seventh Sephirah, is associated with the number seven and represents victory or triumph. The eighth Sephirah, Hod, is associated with the number eight and represents glory or splendor.

The ninth Sephirah, Yesod, is associated with the number nine and represents foundation or stability. The tenth and final Sephirah, Malkuth, is associated with the number ten and represents kingdom or domain.

Example Readings

When you understand the meaning of each Sephirah, you can begin to see how the numerical correspondences of the Minor Arcana can be used to interpret the hidden meanings of a Tarot reading.

For example, if you are using a Swords-based deck and draw the Ace of Swords, this card would represent the Divine will or purpose (Kether) manifesting in the world of form (Assiah).

Suppose you use a Cups-based deck and draw the Ace of Cups. This card would represent the Divine will or purpose (Kether) manifesting in the world of emotion or feeling (Briah). In a reading, this card could indicate that you are about to experience a great influx of emotions or that you are about to embark on a new emotional journey.

If you are using a Wands-based deck, and you draw the Ace of Wands, this card would represent the Divine will or purpose (Kether) manifesting in the world of formation (Yetzirah). In a reading, these cards would indicate that something new is about to enter your life and that you have the power to shape it according to your own will.

The Tree of Life is a powerful tool for understanding the hidden meanings of the Tarot. By studying the Sephirot and their numerical correspondences, you can unlock the secrets of the Minor Arcana and gain a deeper insight into their role in a Tarot reading.

Chapter 10: Daily Kabalistic Rituals and Ideas

Kabbalah is a system of esoteric knowledge that includes principles and practices designed to help people achieve union with the divine. The Tree of Life is a central symbol in Kabbalah, representing the structure of the cosmos and the path that leads to ultimate reality. Kabbalists believe that the Tree of Life is a map of reality and a blueprint for creation. The Tree of Life is a symbol of the interconnectedness of all things. It is said to contain all the secrets of the universe. Kabbalists also believe the Tree of Life is a tool for spiritual growth, and by studying it, we can learn how to create our reality.

The Shabbat is also a time for performing special rituals, such as lighting candles and saying blessings over bread and wine.
https://www.pexels.com/photo/close-up-photo-of-candle-holder-on-top-of-glass-table-6115411/

Practicing Kabbalah can help us connect with the Divine and to lead more meaningful and productive lives. Many different Kabbalistic rituals and ideas can be incorporated into our daily lives. This chapter will explore some of the most popular Kabbalistic practices. It will also guide you through the ideal way to read and study the sacred texts of Kabbalah. With this knowledge, you'll be able to start incorporating Kabbalistic principles into your own life and begin your journey toward spiritual growth.

Daily Kabalistic Rituals and Ideas

Keeping the Kabbalistic Tree of Life in mind when performing your daily rituals is crucial. The Tree of Life is a representation of the universe, and by understanding its components, you can better understand the universe's workings and apply them to your own life. There are 10 Sephiroth on the Tree of Life, each representing a different aspect of existence. By meditating on these and including them in your daily rituals, you'll begin to imbue your life with the wisdom of the Kabbalah.

Some things to keep in mind when performing your rituals:

1. Always start with the Sephirah at the bottom of the tree and work your way up.

2. Make sure your thoughts and actions are aligned with each Sephirah.

3. Be patient and diligent in your practice; it may take time to see results.

4. Enjoy the journey, and let the wisdom of the Kabbalah guide you on your path.

The following are some daily rituals and ideas that you can incorporate into your life:

The Morning Prayer

The morning prayer is a great way to start the day with the Kabalistic Tree of Life in mind. By consecrating each day with this prayer, we begin to infuse our days and lives with the wisdom of the Kabbalah. The morning prayer is as follows:

"Blessed are You, Lord our God, King of the universe, who has sanctified us with His commandments and commanded us to pray.

God, in Your goodness, please incline Your ear and hear my prayer.

I arise today through Your grace and power. May I be filled with love and compassion for all living creatures? Let me perform good deeds today that will bring me closer to You. Help me to see the good in everyone I meet, and let me always be forgiving. Guide my thoughts and actions so that I may always do that which is pleasing unto You. Amen."

The Evening Prayer

One of the most important ways to connect with the wisdom of the Kabalistic tree of life is by performing daily rituals that honor its teachings. One such ritual is the evening prayer. This prayer helps to align oneself with the energy of the day and sets the tone for a peaceful and productive evening.

You will need a piece of paper and a pen or pencil to perform the evening prayer. Begin by sitting comfortably and taking a few deep breaths to calm your mind. Once you are relaxed, write down the following words:

"Dear God, thank you for this day and all it has brought. Thank you for your love, guidance, and protection. Please help me to align myself with your will for this evening. Amen."

Once you have written down the prayer, take a few minutes to focus on each word and what it means to you. As you do, open yourself up to feel the peace and calm that comes from connecting with God. When you are finished, fold up the paper and place it somewhere near your bed, where you can see it before going to sleep.

The Shabbat

The Shabbat is a special day of rest and contemplation in the Jewish tradition. It begins at sundown on Friday night and lasts until nightfall on Saturday. During this time, Jews refrained from work and devoted themselves to prayer, study, and spending time with family and friends. The Shabbat is also a time for performing special rituals, such as lighting candles and saying blessings over bread and wine.

These rituals help to create a sense of peace and tranquility, which can be especially beneficial during times of stress or turmoil. They also serve as a reminder of how necessary it is to slow down and take time to appreciate the simplest things in life. For Jews, the Shabbat is a sacred day – meant to be enjoyed and savored.

The New Moon

The New Moon is a time of new beginnings and the perfect time to perform some daily Kabalistic rituals. One simple ritual is to light a white candle and visualize your highest goal. As you focus on your intention, allow the candle's flame to represent the power of your desire. Another ritual is to write down your goals for the month ahead. Be specific and realistic in your intentions, and then let go of any attachment to the outcome.

Trust that the universe will support you in achieving your goals. Lastly, take some time on the New Moon to meditate and connect with your inner wisdom. Listen for guidance from your higher self, and trust that you are being supported on your journey. By taking some time to connect with the energy of the New Moon, you can set yourself up for success in the month ahead.

Passover

The Passover holiday is a time for Kabbalists to reflect on their spiritual journey and connect with their higher selves. One of the ways they do this is through daily rituals that help them to attune to the energies of the universe. One such ritual is the Seder, a ceremonial meal with special foods and prayers.

The Seder helps Kabbalists to remember the importance of liberation, both physical and spiritual. Another important ritual is counting the Omer, which is 49 days of introspection and meditation. The Omer helps Kabbalists to connect with their power and focus on their goals. By participating in these daily rituals, Kabbalists can deepen their connection to the divine and create a more fulfilling life.

The High Holy Days

The High Holy Days are some of the most important days in the Kabalistic calendar. These days, Kabbalists perform special cleansing and purification rituals and ask for forgiveness from the Divine. The first of the High Holy Days is Rosh Hashanah, which marks the beginning of the Jewish New Year. On Rosh Hashanah, Kabbalists gather together to pray and meditate. They also perform a special ritual known as Tashlikh, in which they cast their sins into a body of water.

The second High Holy Day is Yom Kippur - or the Day of Atonement. On Yom Kippur, Kabbalists fast and spend the day in prayer and contemplation. They also perform the rite of Kol Nidre, in which they repent for their past sins. These special rituals help Kabbalists to start the year anew with a clean slate and a deep connection to the Divine.

Sukkot

Sukkot is a seven-day festival that occurs in the fall. It is also known as the Feast of Tabernacles or the Feast of Ingathering. During Sukkot, Jews built temporary huts, or sukkahs, and ate all their meals inside them. The sukkah symbolizes the huts the Israelites lived in during their forty years in the desert.

Each day of Sukkot has its special rituals and observances. On the first day, Jews built their sukkahs and decorated them with fruits and vegetables. They also wave palm fronds and myrtle branches in six different directions, symbolizing the six directions of space. Special prayers and readings from the Torah are recited on the second day. On the third day, they offer sacrifices at the Temple in Jerusalem. And on the fourth day, they celebrate Hoshana Rabbah, which is when they praise God for His bountiful blessings.

Sukkot is a joyous occasion, but it is also a time for reflection. Jews remember their dependence on God's mercy and protection during this holiday. They also reflect on the importance of treating others with kindness and compassion. Sukkot is a time to celebrate our lives and all we have been blessed with while also remembering those less fortunate.

Daily Life with the Tree of Life

Meditation

We can use the Tree of Life as a guide for our daily meditation practice. For example, we can focus on one Sephira daily and meditate on its meaning and significance. Alternatively, we can choose to meditate on the path between two Sephiroth or on the entire Tree of Life itself. Kabalistic meditation is a powerful tool for self-discovery and growth, and the Tree of Life is an excellent map to help us on our journey.

Readings

Another way to permeate our daily lives with the grace of the Tree of Life is to select readings related to its symbolism and meaning. Many books are available, and Kabalistic texts often contain references to its Sephiroth. By reading about the Tree of Life, we get a deeper understanding of its wisdom and how it can help us to live more fulfilling lives.

Reciting Prayers

Prayer is a vital part of Kabalistic practice, and the Tree of Life can be a helpful guide for our prayer life. For example, we can recite prayers associated with specific Sephiroth or use the Tree of Life as a visualization tool during our prayers. We can deepen our connection to its wisdom and power by including the Tree of Life in our prayers.

Using the Tree of Life in the Creation of Future Goals

The Tree of Life can also be helpful to use when we want to set future goals. By understanding the symbolism of the Sephiroth, we can use them as guideposts on our journey toward our highest aspirations. By aligning our goals with the energies of the Tree of Life, we can increase our chances of achieving them.

Using the Kabbalistic System of Creation

The Kabbalistic creation system is useful for taking an idea from its raw, shapeless state (Keter) and transforming it into physical reality (Malkuth). Working through the ten Sephiroth stages of creation makes it possible to give form and substance to an idea, making it increasingly concrete and tangible. The ten Sephiroth is a hierarchy, with each stage building on the one before it. For example, the first stage, Keter, is the purest and most abstract form of an idea. As the idea moves down through the Sephiroth, it becomes increasingly refined and specific until it reaches Malkuth, the final stage, in which it takes on a physical form. Using the Kabbalistic system of creation, it is possible to bring even the most ephemeral idea into reality.

Sacred Kabbalistic Texts and How to Read Them

The Sefer Yetzirah

The Sefer Yetzirah is one of the most sacred texts in the Kabbalah tradition. It contains wisdom on how to create and interpret sacred Jewish texts. To read and understand the Sefer Yetzirah properly, it is crucial to have a basic understanding of the Hebrew alphabet. Each letter has a numerical value, which can be used to interpret the meaning of words and phrases. The Sefer Yetzirah also contains a great deal of symbolism, which can be difficult to interpret without guidance from a knowledgeable teacher. However, even a basic understanding of the text can provide insight into the depths of the Kabbalistic tradition. With proper study and practice, anyone can learn to read and understand the Sefer Yetzirah.

Zohar

There are many different sacred texts in the Jewish Kabbalistic tradition, and each has its unique purpose and teachings. The Zohar is perhaps the best-known and most studied of these texts – and is considered the *cornerstone of Kabbalistic wisdom*. The Zohar contains mystical secrets and insights into the nature of God, the universe, and the human soul. To properly understand and benefit from its teachings, it is necessary to approach the text with reverence and respect.

The Zohar is traditionally divided into five sections or books. Each section contains several chapters, or paragraphs, further divided into smaller units called paragraphs. In addition, each section has a specific color associated with it, which helps to guide the reader through the text. For example, the first book is connected with the color red, which symbolizes fire and passion. The second book is yellow, which represents wisdom and clarity. The third book is green, related to growth and fertility, while the fourth book is blue, connected with truth and understanding. Finally, the fifth book is purple, associated with royalty and power.

By taking the time to understand the structure and symbolism of the Zohar, readers can begin to unlock its secrets and gain deeper insight into its mystical teachings.

Bahir

The Bahir is a sacred text that has been used for centuries to help people connect with the divine. The word "Bahir" means "illumination," and the text is designed to help readers understand the universe and their place within it. It is divided into three sections, each of which contains a series of meditations, stories, and exercises. The first section, known as the "Practical Kabbalah," offers guidance on how to live a spiritual life.

The second section, known as the "Mystical Kabbalah," helps readers explore the nature of reality. The third section, known as the "Esoteric Kabbalah," helps readers understand the relationship between God and man. While the Bahir is not easy to read, it is considered essential for those who wish to deepen their understanding of the Kabbalah.

PaRDeS

The PaRDeS approach is a method of text interpretation that has its roots in Jewish Kabbalah. The acronym PaRDeS stands for four different levels of interpretation: peshat, remez, drash, and sod. Peshat is the text's literal meaning, while Remez is the allegorical meaning. Drash is the interpretive meaning, and sod is the hidden or mystical meaning. PaRDeS was first developed as a way to interpret sacred texts, but it can also be used when interpreting any type of written work.

When using the PaRDeS approach, readers first identify which level of interpretation they are looking for. They then read the text closely, looking for clues that will help them to unlock its meaning. Depending on the level they are aiming for, readers may need to look beyond the literal meaning of the words on the page and explore the hidden symbolism and allegorical meanings. By taking the time to unpack all four levels of interpretation, readers can gain a deeper understanding of any written work – from ancient religious texts to modern novels.

Kabbalah is a complex and mysterious tradition that religious scholars have studied for centuries. While it can be difficult to understand, the rewards for those who take the time to study it are great. By understanding the structure and symbolism of key Kabbalistic texts, such as the Zohar and the Bahir, readers can unlock the secrets of this ancient tradition and gain deeper insight into its teachings.

In addition, the PaRDeS approach to text interpretation can help readers understand any type of written work, from sacred texts to modern novels. By taking the time to explore all four levels of interpretation, readers can gain a greater understanding of the hidden meanings that lie beneath the surface of any text.

Extra: Glossary of Terms

Kabbalah is an ancient wisdom that reveals how to create harmony and balance in our lives. It is a system of knowledge that helps us to reach our highest potential and create the life we truly desire. This book introduced you to the basics of Kabbalah, its history, and how it can help you in your own life. This chapter will provide a brief glossary of terms for your convenience.

- **Ain Soph:** The Unknowable Godhead, the infinite light that is the source of all creation.

- **Ain Soph Aur:** The infinite light of God that is manifest in creation.

- **Atzilut:** The world of emanation, the highest of the four spiritual worlds.

- **Binah:** Understanding. In Kabbalah, Binah is the third sefirah and is considered the highest form of understanding.

- **Beriyah:** The world of creation, the second of the four spiritual worlds.

- **Butzina deKala:** The feminine aspect of God.

- **Chakra:** A spinning wheel of energy located in the body. There are 7 main chakras in the body, each associated with a different area and function.

- **Chesed:** Lovingkindness. In Kabbalah, Chesed is the fourth sefirah and is considered the highest expression of love.
- **Chokhmah:** Wisdom. In Kabbalah, Chokhmah is the second sefirah and is considered the highest form of wisdom.
- **Da'at:** Knowledge. In Kabbalah, Da'at is the tenth sefirah and is considered the highest form of knowledge. Through Da'at, we can attain a true understanding of the universe.
- **Ein Sof:** The unknowable Godhead, the infinite light that is the source of all creation. In Kabbalah, Ein Sof is often referred to as the "Ain Soph Aur" or the "Infinite Light of God."
- **Elyon:** The highest or most exalted one. In Kabbalah, Elyon refers to God as the supreme being who is above all else.
- **Gan Eden:** The Garden of Eden, the paradise that awaits us after we die.
- **Gehinnom:** The Jewish concept of hell.
- **Gevurah:** Strength or power. In Kabbalah, Gevurah is the fifth sefirah and is considered the highest expression of strength.
- **Hokhmah:** Wisdom. In Kabbalah, Hokhmah is the first sefirah and is considered the highest form of wisdom.
- **Hod:** Splendor. In Kabbalah, Hod is the eighth sefirah and is considered to be the highest expression of splendor.
- **Kabbalist:** A student or practitioner of Kabbalah.
- **Malchut:** The kingdom or realm. In Kabbalah, Malchut refers to the physical world, which is the lowest of the four spiritual worlds.
- **Merkabah:** In Kabbalah, the Merkabah is a symbol of our own journey to enlightenment. The Merkabah is the divine light vehicle used by the prophet Ezekiel to ascend to heaven. It is said that the Merkabah can help us attain our highest potential and connect with the divine.
- **Netzach:** Victory. In Kabbalah, Netzach is the seventh sefirah and is considered the highest expression of victory.

- **Olam HaBa:** The world to come, the afterlife. It is said that in Olam HaBa, we will be reunited with our loved ones who have passed on.

- **Olam HaZeh:** This world, the physical world. The lowest of the four spiritual worlds.

- **Pardes:** In Kabbalah, Pardes refers to the four levels of interpretation of scripture. The four levels are literal, allegorical, moral, and anagogical.

- **Raḥamim:** Compassion. In Kabbalah, Raḥamim is the ninth sefirah and is considered to be the highest expression of compassion.

- **Sefirot:** The 10 divine attributes or emanations of God used to create and sustain the universe.

- **Shekinah:** The divine presence of God. In Kabbalah, the Shekinah is often represented as a feminine aspect of God.

- **Shevirah:** The act of breaking or shattering. In Kabbalah, Shevirah refers to the moment when God created the universe by shattering the vessel that contained His infinite light. This act of divine creation resulted in the separation of the light from the darkness, which gave birth to the universe as we know it.

- **Tiferet:** Beauty. In Kabbalah, Tiferet is the sixth sefirah and is considered to be the highest expression of beauty.

- **Tikkun:** The process of repairing or mending. In Kabbalah, Tikkun refers to the process of repairing the world and restoring it to its original state of perfection.

- **Tzimtzum:** The act of self-contraction or withdrawal. In Kabbalah, Tzimtzum refers to the moment God withdrew His light to create the universe.

- **Yesod:** The foundation. In Kabbalah, Yesod is the ninth sefirah and is considered to be the foundation of all reality.

- **Zohar:** The central text of Kabbalah, which contains the mystical teachings of Rabbi Shimon bar Yochai.

Conclusion

As we have seen, Kabbalah is a mystical tradition with ancient roots. It teaches that we can access hidden knowledge and power by attaining a deep understanding of the divine nature of reality. Kabbalah also provides a powerful framework for understanding the human psyche and our place in the cosmos. Despite its great age, Kabbalah remains a living tradition that continues to evolve and grow. In recent years, it has experienced a resurgence of interest, with many people from all walks of life drawn to its wisdom.

In this guide on Kabbalah, we have explored some key concepts and practices that make up this tradition. We have looked at its history and how it has developed over time. We have also considered what it takes to become a Kabbalist and how Kabbalah can be used in our daily lives.

The Tree of Life is a central symbol, and we have spent some time exploring its meaning and significance. We have also looked at the Sephirot, the different levels of reality described by Kabbalah, and the role of the archangels in this tradition. From the Supernal Triad to the Ethical Triad and the Minor Arcana, Kabbalah provides us with a rich and detailed map of reality.

As we have seen, Kabbalah, complex and multifaceted, offers us a way to understand the world around us and where we fit in. By delving deeper into Kabbalah, we can better understand ourselves and the universe we inhabit. At the end of this guide, we explored some of the daily practices and rituals associated with Kabbalah. These are just a few of the many ways in which this tradition can enrich our lives.

Whether you are just beginning your exploration of Kabbalah or already well-versed in its teachings, we hope this guide has provided you with some valuable insights.

Kabbalah is a complex and rich tradition with much to offer to those willing to engage with it. We encourage you to continue your journey of discovery and wish you every success on your kabbalistic path. This informative guide has provided you with a brief introduction to Kabbalah. Hopefully, it has whetted your appetite to explore this rich and fascinating tradition further. There are many excellent books and resources available to help you on your journey of discovery. With an open mind and heart, Kabbalah can provide you with a lifetime of wisdom and insights. So, why not start your Kabbalistic journey today?

Here's another book by Silvia Hill that you might like

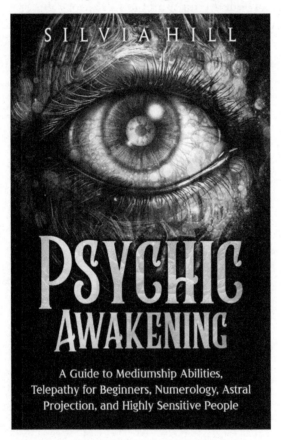

Free Bonus from Silvia Hill available for limited time

Hi Spirituality Lovers!

My name is Silvia Hill, and first off, I want to THANK YOU for reading my book.

Now you have a chance to join my exclusive spirituality email list so you can get the ebooks below for free as well as the potential to get more spirituality ebooks for free! Simply click the link below to join.

P.S. Remember that it's 100% free to join the list.

~~$27~~ FREE BONUSES

 9 Types of Spirit Guides and How to Connect to Them

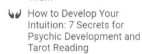 How to Develop Your Intuition: 7 Secrets for Psychic Development and Tarot Reading

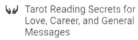 Tarot Reading Secrets for Love, Career, and General Messages

Access your free bonuses here
https://livetolearn.lpages.co/jewish-magic-and-kabbalah-paperback/

References

Ariel, D. S. (1977). The mystic quest: An introduction to Jewish mysticism. Jason Aronson, Incorporated.

Besserman, P. (2018). Kabbalah: The way of the Jewish mystic (Vol. 24). Shambhala Publications.

Blumenthal, D. R. (Ed.). (1978). Understanding Jewish mysticism: A source reader. KTAV Publishing House, Inc.

Elior, R. (2004). The Three Temples: On the Emergence of Jewish Mysticism. Liverpool University Press.

Frankiel, T., & Greenfeld, J. (1997). Minding the temple of the soul: Balancing body, mind, and spirit through traditional Jewish prayer, movement, and meditation. Jewish Lights Publishing.

Ginsburgh, R. Y. (1990). The Hebrew letters: Channels of creative consciousness (Vol. 1). GalEinai Publication Society.

Ginsburg, Y., Trugman, A. A., & Wisnefsky, M. Y. (1991). The Alef-Beit: Jewish Thought Revealed through the Hebrew Letters. Rowman & Littlefield.

Green, A. (2014). Keter: The Crown of God in Early Jewish Mysticism (Vol. 366). Princeton University Press.

Haralick, R. M. (1995). Inner Meaning of the Hebrew Letters. Jason Aronson, Incorporated.

Rowland, C., & Morray-Jones, C. R. (2009). The Mystery of God: Early Jewish Mysticism and the New Testament. Brill.

Schäfer, P. (2011). The origins of Jewish mysticism. Princeton University Press.

Schafer, P. (2012). Hidden and Manifest God, The: Some Major Themes in Early Jewish Mysticism. SUNY Press.

Scholem, G. (1967). Jewish mysticism. Merkabah Mysticism and Talmudic Tradition

Kerstein, B. (2018). Kabbalah. World History Encyclopedia. https://www.worldhistory.org/Kabbalah/

My Jewish Learning. (2003, February 10). Kabbalah and mysticism 101. My Jewish Learning. https://www.myjewishlearning.com/article/Kabbalah-mysticism-101/

The Editors of Encyclopedia Britannica. (2022). Kabbala. In Encyclopedia Britannica.

What is Kabbalah? (2014). In Kabbalah: A Guide for The Perplexed. Continuum.

(N.d.-a). Labyrinthos.Co. https://labyrinthos.co/blogs/learn-tarot-with-labyrinthos-academy/the-tarot-and-the-tree-of-life-correspondences#:~:text=The%20nodes%20of%20the%20Tree,closer%20and%20closer%20to%20manifestation.

(N.d.-b). Chabad.org. https://www.chabad.org/library/article_cdo/aid/170308/jewish/What-is-Kabbalah.htm

Printed in Great Britain
by Amazon

37360283R00126